CHRISTINE
a memoir

Christine Spittel Wilson

Perera Hussein Publishing House

Published by the Perera Hussein Publishing House, 2007
ISBN: 955-8897-12-4
First Edition 2007

The right of the author to be associated with this work has been asserted.
© Christine Spittel Wilson
Photographs : from the author's private collection
Printed and bound in Sri Lanka by Samayawardhana

To offset the environmental pollution caused in printing books,
the Perera Hussein Publishing House grows trees in Puttalam,
in Sri Lanka's semi-arid zone.

CHRISTINE

a memoir

Also by Christine Spittel Wilson

The Bitter Berry
Bittere Bere (German)
Tea Plantations in Ceylon
The Mountain Road
D*ie Strasse Nach Kaschmir*
I am the Wings
Growing Up, and other stories,
Reach For The Stars
The Priest and The Python
Surgeon of the Wilderness
Brave Island (with R.L.Spittel)

Secrets of Eastern Cooking

Under the *nom de plume* Frances Neil :
Love Must Go On

With love I dedicate this book to Alistair, my husband for 62 years and thank him for his endless help and encouragement.

This is my aim:
To leave some lasting tribute to this land I love
Changes of mood and scene,
Remembered scent of wood-smoke rising on an evening breeze;
Bird-song and wind-song mingle midst forest trees;
Strange ways and byways, which once were hard and sore,
New ways and old ways that man had walked before.
These I have known and cared for in my island long ago
But the old ways now are shattered
I know not where to go.
Tsunami's claw at our coast line,
The Teeth of Tigers show.
But deep hidden – Dear God, where? –
Still lies Sri Lanka's essence.
Indestructible, most rare.

Last night I dreamed I saw Kaira again. He stood before me as he had stood long ago, bare-bodied, his wild hair clotted on his shoulders, his skin greyed with the dust of ages, and even in my dream I saw, above all, the wild eyes with the look of a stricken animal. The child my father had saved from the jungle and brought home to be my playmate.

I shake the vision from my thoughts. Outside my window two crow pheasants call, the deep note of the male answered by the softer one of the female. At some time during the day the two calls will come from a single branch, but now, a Koha joins them with a different song. So thoughts come and go, each reiterating in some way the other. The past slides into view, clear, clearer than the present.

1913-1930

A Writer is Born

Shadow owes its birth to light
- John Gay -

I CAN NO LONGER find the house, or rather the annexe where my little sister and I were born. Alexandra Place, the road on which it stood, is three times as wide as it used to be; its houses trapped within high walls and iron gates. Opposite, Victoria Park - now the Vihara Mahadevi Park - is a third less than its original size, its lawns blurred by kiosks, buildings, playgrounds, but still a green haven in the ever-more demanding city of Colombo.

My mind holds a swirl of memories of my island, Ceylon, as it was then.

My earliest memory: My mother, father, and I with unruly curls, thin, happy. *Dear God,* I used to pray, *I am so happy. Please let me die young.* What instinct made me use those words I do not know. There wasn't much money. My father's salary as a senior surgeon of the General Hospital, Colombo, was Rs. 750 a month. But we were happy. Even with the torment of a frozen shoulder, a physical frailness he would bear all his life, vitality surged through him. My mother, beautiful, unpractical, a physician herself, was the perfect companion for him intellectually and she adored him unequivocally. Only one thing puzzled me.

Twice a year, when the heat sucked the rivers dry and the rasp of the cicadas was harsh in the land, my father would disappear into unknown forests, for what reason I did not know. When he returned, exhausted, disgracefully unkempt but jubilant, he would tell tales of a jungle I could not imagine; he showed us photographs of a dying people I never guessed I would learn to care for.

❧

When the sun burned its way into late afternoon and the land shimmered with the dust rising, I'd sit on the steps of the annexe in Alexandra Place and wait. The road would be empty then except for a carriage or a rickshaw pulled by turbaned men from whose thudding feet rose drifts of fine red dust. Beyond lay Victoria Park with copses of great flowering trees, tailored lawns and a bandstand where blue uniformed men blared patriotic British music to unheeding nannies and children. Then, at the first faint clonk of the wooden bell I'd run to the gate, sandals skittering.

The water cart, drawn by an amiable humped bull, came slowly. From a punctured drum, filaments of rainbowed water arched over the road and ran in cool, dark rivulets to my toes. Years later, boiling tar drowned the red road and steamrollers pressed granite chips and sand to make tarmac roadways for cars instead of carriages.

❧

Ceylon then was a land of forests and jungles. Countless waterfalls ran unharnessed from its hills; there were secret coves and undiscovered caves; far-away beaches gemmed with coral and rare shells, vast tanks and a web of an irrigation system a thousand years old. The past still lingered in a Portuguese fort here, in a remnant of a fiercely defended Dutch fort there. Tramways drove through Colombo's main street and beyond them were the crowded boutiques of the Pettah where neat, elbow-nudging Dutch houses with courtyards had stood. In one of these, an ancestor of my mother's had lived a century ago.

In the central massif, there lay forest greened hilltops - five, six thousand feet high, their valleys cobwebbed with ancient man-made waterways. To the Northeast on the map lay a vast road-less region marked, *Wanni - Vedda Territory,* where a forgotten fragment of aborigines hunted their food, and my father hunted, alone, for their beginnings.

❧

Our small annexe was a beginning, its size unimportant against its proximity to the General Hospital, where my father, the third surgeon in the island to get his Fellowship, had his consulting practice.

I see him, forever frail from the months of surgery to save his arm from septicaemia. Restless, angry with himself, impatient, he knew he must conserve the raw energy pulsing inside him to make up for lost time; plan each moment of each day to be productive. It now seems strange to me that it was my gentle mother who had been the driving force that first dared him to do what devoured him; it was she who had given him the book, Seligmann's *The Veddas,* the dying tribe that he made his main objective in life to record. Now and forever, with little physical strength, he knew he must harness time. From then on he worked to a strict schedule, a time for everything from sunrise into dark.

The skinny child with her curls tied up with ribbon on either side of her forehead knew nothing of these complications. Life was fun; it was beautiful where shadow-land pixies thrown against a white wall danced on wind-quivering antignon creepers and mushrooms sprang in a magic circle on dew-fresh grass.

Sometimes, unknown to my parents, I walked demurely barefoot across the garden to visit at the large house adjoining our annexe. Its owner, a widower, had recently married an eighteen-year old bride. Every evening he lay dressed in spotless white, his legs stretched on his long-chair, his coffee-cream soles above neatly laid slippers. Beside him in a shimmering saree his new wife sat, hands folded, eyes demurely downcast. Her oval face with a single small diamond at one delicate nostril was as smooth as soft brown suede, with an almost invisible down. Sometimes she wore a cobweb line of kohl on her eyes that made them look as timorous as a deer's. When I visited, she'd rise and taking my hand, lead me into the dining room to offer some special sweetmeat scented with cardamoms, a drink of island oranges. She smelled of a curiously scented blend of sweet oils; her hair fell in a glowing rope into which she idly threaded fresh jasmine. She'd watch me wistfully. Though neither spoke the other's language, we shared the unity of a kind of loneliness.

I write of a shadow child that was myself; a child of remembered yesterdays who had no consciousness of a land that would change beyond recognition.

When I returned from my visit, my mother would say sadly, "Bunting, please don't walk about without your sandals." If my father was around he'd say, "Let her run free. It's good for her." He encouraged me to climb the low-lying *num-num* tree, to jump from steps onto gritty hot sand below, to look at every moving thing and tell him and my mother about it. But best of all were *his* stories. When the last patient had gone, and Podian our young Tamil help had stopped waving his incense burner to discourage mosquitoes, I'd sit on the cement floor by my father's chair and listen. He made me see campfires glistening on strange, dark faces; hear the grunt of harsh voices that spoke another tongue, and when all was still he'd speak of other voices of the jungle night where unseen creatures moved. "See, Bunting! In the dappled moonlight, something moves - a leopard?"

At the far side of our garden was *my* forest.

At William's garden where plants were sold, only a sagging barbed-wire fence separated our two properties. Inside, inter-arching avenues of potted foliage and ferns feathered my face as I moved to and fro under them like a puppy that brushes its coat against its beloved. This was my forest like the jungles my father visited. A dragonfly hovered over a barrel of water. A small striped squirrel chirruped piercingly and was still. A red chameleon tightroped its way along the red stem of some unknown plant. These were my creatures. My father, I thought, was a chameleon person. My mother, once so beautiful – what was she?

When my father came home from hospital, I'd skip up the steps with him to the veranda where my mother waited.

"How did it go to-day, Dick? A heavy operation day?"

He nods, too tired to speak.

"Shoulder hurting?"

He will not admit it. Instead he withdraws into himself, his shoulder scrunched into his body; he fights the pain; reading poetry, philosophy, the Classics, letting the beauty of words or great thoughts act as an anodyne.

I had grown up with the story of the scars that ran up his operating arm and crumpled into his shoulder; knew the saga of endless pain he suffered after he returned from England with his fellowship and developed virulent septicaemia from an operation he had done at the General Hospital. My mother had been there for him, through nine months of screaming agony as operation after operation bit into his arm, while he drifted in and out of consciousness. He had walked out with a permanently damaged operating arm, but she had helped him refocus in a way that changed not only his own life but also that of a lost people hidden deep in the jungle.

As night falls, light touches my mother's softly wavy hair, touches the austere planes of my father's face with the quirky smile. There is the heady scent of the lime-green blossoms of the *Ruk-Athana* tree in the garden, where on *Poya* nights of the full moon a small Scops-owl calls and next day flowers carpet the grass below.

෴

Another day, my father is watching me blowing bubbles, a smile on his face.

"Suppose the clay pipe breaks?" I ask him.

"Use a straw, child of my heart. A hollow leaf stalk if you can't find anything else; or blow a bubble through the circle of your thumb and forefinger – there are always answers. If not exactly the one you want, move on to something else."

I was tired of blowing bubbles. I'd broken the clay pipe, there were no dry hollow leafstalks to blow them through and no bubble would blow through the circle of my finger and thumb.

"It's not true, what you told me!"

"It is, you know. I told you if you can't find the right answers, move on to something else."

"Why do you go to the jungles?"

"Because there are a forgotten people, my dear, who will die if I don't do something about it."

❧

"Come, Bunting," my mother said one day. "We're going to visit Grandfather."

"I don't want to visit Grandfather," I said. He was at least a hundred years old.

Grandfather Van Dort

Seated in his curved ebony chair upstairs, his long white beard and shaggy eyebrows even whiter than I remembered, Grandfather van Dort dominated the room. I stared at the heavy gold watch and chain across his chest while he patted my head absent-mindedly. "Takes after her father," he remarked, sighing. "How old is the child?"

"Five. Dick's off again soon to visit his Veddas. Father, I worry about him so much."

"You take care of yourself, Claribel, my dearest child," said my grandfather forgetting me. "Having a baby at forty-three…" I had escaped to look at the Motorola to which he sometimes let me listen and barely heard what he said.

❧

Dick, do you remember…? Maybe she was remembering medical school in Colombo before they went abroad for further qualifications. She was the fourth woman doctor to get her physician's qualifications at Edinburgh University. And afterwards then what…?

At dusk one day, my father took me to visit the ward where he had been. We walked together down long cemented verandas separated from other wards where patients lay in two rows of beds. We didn't speak, and in our silence I was aware of the smell of disinfectant, the sharper smell of sickness, the soft moans of patients, a sudden desperate cry that went on and on, and as suddenly ceased. In the wards, white-cowled nuns greeted him quietly.

"It was here I fell in love with your mother again. She nursed me through months of pain. Very few people know what a wonderful person she is behind her quietness. Anything I am today, my dear, is because of her."

MY MOTHER WAS BORN on April 17th 1876 in Colombo. Her father Dr. William Gregory van Dort, originally from Utrecht, Holland and in the services of the Dutch East India Company, first married the Countess Lechenstein, a widow, who died shortly afterwards. He gained his medical degrees in Aberdeen, then travelled widely on the Continent, had a working knowledge of seven languages, and a group of literary friends including Dickens with whom he corresponded. His second marriage was to Sophia McCarthy, daughter of an English mother and an Irish father, who was a lay priest in the Baptist church. She bore him eight children of whom two died and Clarie was the favourite.

Clarie grew up with one sister Aline and four brothers. The girls had a governess and the boys a tutor. When they were older the children were taken by their mother Sophie to England for their education. They lived in St. Leonards–on–Sea and while Aline who was delicate schooled at home, Clarie went to the prestigious Cheltenham Ladies College, known for its advanced education. Clarie didn't speak much about her early childhood but did mention that they had a lot of discipline, rules and church even though her father was an atheist. She once told me of a journey on the Bridge of Boats that crossed the Kelaniya river and the large and beautiful Beira Lake.

At Cheltenham Ladies College, Miss Popham, the Headmistress recommended that she study medicine, probably influenced by Florence Nightingale. Claribel went on to become the second woman to be accepted into the Colombo Medical College. It was there that she first met my father, Richard Spittel, himself the son of a country doctor whose ancestors came from Weimar, Saxony, and who themselves joined the Dutch East India Company. At the Medical College in Colombo, Richard fell immediately in love with Clarie. In their finals she won the gold medal for Surgery where she had to study the newly decapitated head of a murderer for her examination.

Clarie wearing a black skirt with Dick standing behind her left shoulder at the graduation of the Medical College

Clarie grew up to be a gentle woman and yet not genteel. Well-mannered but not obsessive about it in others. Her great weakness was that she was over-sensitive, and had great love for Richard and her daughter.

I have two different kinds of love for my parents. Each quite distinct from the other; and I was part of each and yet not the whole. With my mother I was the nicely-brought-up little girl with my hair combed up with two perky ribbons, and *Thank-you-very-much-for-the-nice-party*. With my father it was, *Ooh Daddy, WHY can't I run barefoot? WHY can't you take me to the jungles?* For Christmas, my mother filled a pillow case with beautifully tied-up presents - lots of books always. My father forgot to give anything but diaries he had been sent, or perhaps a box of chocolates from the hampers that shops like Millers and Cargills liked to send at Christmas-time.

I AM BEATING WITH small, impotent fists at a locked door. "Let me in!" I scream. But no one answers. Inside there are noises, voices, sudden silences. "Let me in!" I scream again. But the door stares back at me. "Dadddy-yy! Daddy!" The door opens a crack and my father, tall, gaunt, says angrily to Jane, my ayah, "Take the child next door," and disappears inside again. From the room I hear my mother scream, then a profound silence as I am dragged away sobbing.

That day my little sister, Yvonne was born, and inside the room with the locked door my mother lay, nearly dying. Everything changed, then.

Earlier that day Grandfather van Dort arrived in his carriage; my father drove back from hospital, his tyres screaming. Through all this my sister came into the world, one small, lovely newcomer. Now our quiet house centred on Yvonne. She was an ivory child, with hazel eyes, soft smile and a light brown curl that brushed her forehead. Everyone adored her, including Jane, who complained, "Miss Christine now very naughty." My mother had eyes only for her, and I was always sent to "Go and play."

From time to time I seriously studied my baby sister who sat quietly on a pale blue blanket in her playpen, her rose-pink toes petal-curled. I spoke and got no answer except a gurgle, a smile, a finger tenuously held. Solemn, long-lashed eyes regarded me, who was brown, thin, and ordinary. Yvonne had a curious birthmark like a thin black cord round her throat. My ayah told me, "Little sister, like angel, she. That black mark - like God's mark." I had no idea what she meant.

When I was six (Yvonne a year and a half), I was told in shielded voices, that my father had to go on routine study leave to England for six months and that my mother would have to go with him. How could I be made to understand how frail my father

Yvonne, 1920

was, and would always be, assaulted as he was with endless attacks of pleurisy, malaria or tick fever after his visits on foot to his beloved forests? Or my mother's depth of fear for him when he had nearly died of septicaemia years ago?

"We?" Both of them leaving us for six months? God knows what words they used. England – where was it? Why did my mother have to go? How could she leave Yvonne and me? Which was more important to her - the research work he was doing or the small, rounded baby who had never had a days' illness? How long would they be away? As long as a jungle trip? They reply in gobbets, "Study Leave... Promise we'll be back before you know we've gone... Bring you lots of presents."

I was to stay with Grandmother Spittel. Yvonne, they said, was a placid child and would give no trouble and was to go to Aunt Rose, a cousin, and her husband, because Grandmother van Dort was not very well.

Finally, the day came when I was fondly delivered to stay-and-be-good with my father's parents. Yvonne, to the caring cousins. She and I were to be taken together every day for a rickshaw drive with Jane ayah round Victoria Park.

❧

Fortunately I adored my five-foot-nothing grandmother and Weimar, an endearingly disorderly house where unusual aunts, uncles, cousins, and friends came and went with fluttering hands and voices that reminded me of my grandmother's poultry yard. In the red-tiled sitting room, a dozen Dutch chairs primly lined two walls. Seven identically furnished bedrooms shared two bathrooms, intriguingly inlaid with a mosaic of broken Dutch East India Company tiles: fragments of blue windmills, blue roses, and small blue people.

Granny S. was special. She had my unruly curls washed with jungle limes boiled to a soapy thickness with seeds of fenugreek. The days passed and she let me run barefoot, climb fruit trees and eat mulberries until their juice stained my lips purple. The garden was beautiful. There was a tropical Damson with clusters of waxy, pink-and-crimson fruit. Trees laden with produce, and a vanilla vine collected in some steamy jungle, with fleshy leaves and heavy pods. Nestled among them was a shelter for a diminutive mouse deer, terrier-sized, that lived happily in its enclosure for years.

She cooked dreamy treats, using her great-grandmother's long-handled iron pans from Holland. *Ijzer cookis, Poffertjes,* drenched in a lime and honey syrup, waffles, Breudher, a twenty-four egg Christmas cake, made with pyramids of candied fruit, honey and brandy, and heady, home-made ginger-beer and milk wine for her endless stream of visitors.

Grandfather Spittel would lie stretched on the long chair on the veranda. He was a long way from Glasgow where he had studied medicine and his voice had grown guttural with the Jaffna cheroots he constantly smoked. In July he grew ill and I was hurried away to stay with friends by the sea. When I returned Grandpa was gone. And Weimar grieved.

❧

At the van Dort Grandmother's large house, Clairvaux in Cambridge Terrace, ladies called with small gold-edged visiting cards, and Grandmother received them, white gloved hands tidily composed over a neatly corseted waist; her silver-gold hair elegantly upswept; a gold cameo brooch fastened the throat of lawn and handmade lace blouses. On occasional Sundays I had to accompany her in her carriage to the Adventist church where her father had preached. How beautiful she was. How frigid.

In August, again there was a flurry at Weimar, whispered conversation with sideways glances towards me. Heads shaken. Quickly hidden tears.

Yvonne, my baby sister had died. A wrong diagnosis. Every day I waited for the afternoon drive to Victoria Park, it never happened again.

MY MOTHER AND FATHER returned to the island devastated, distanced from each other by the two deaths in the family.

My mother had become a strange, silent person, with drawn cheeks, her hair cut short. Instead of the dresses she had bought in England, she wore drab cottons. When we spoke to her she hardly seemed to hear. I cried and she would begin to cry too each night in a low, monotonous keening that I could hear from the next room.

Where there had been shared conversation our home was now filled with silences; voices raised behind locked doors, then more silence full of smouldering sorrow.

One Saturday I heard my father's step, even more decisive than usual, then his voice and my mother's, high-pitched. I ran to the doorway and stood staring. He was tearing from a large parcel on the table many layers of sodden paper that crumbled and fell in damp flakes on the polished cement floor. A vast book lay exposed, its cover of mildewed greyed black, was of tooled leather with a hand-wrought lock. In a fold of brittle paper was a beautifully wrought brass key. "It's riddled with bookworms," my father said. "We'll have to burn it," as he tried the key.

I heard a strangled cry from my mother. "Oh, please, Dick…!"

Then, too frail to resist, the key turned in the lock.

Feathers of dust fell as he opened the book and I moved close, unnoticed. On the flyleaf, I saw for the first time, beautiful copperplate writing traced with a quill pen in the brown ink of another age. *Cornelis van Dort, born in Utrecht; arrived in the ship de Bellois, 1700.* The history of my mother's family in Zeilan as it was called by the Dutch. The last item, entered in a different ink, inscribed the marriage of my grandfather's favourite daughter, *Claribel Frances van Dort to Richard Lionel Spittel, F.R.C.S., London.* What I saw then, and was too young fully to understand, I can see now as clearly as if the page was before me: below, in my mother's handwriting, was the date of my own birth, and below again, but in smudged ink, the birth and death dates of my little sister Yvonne, aged two.

That year, a few months later, Grandmother van Dort died, and a fortnight later, my grandfather. Most of my grandfather's once-great fortune had gone to pay his son Herbert's debts in Kuala Lumpur, where he had bought bogus, 'salted' goldmines. Double death duties wiped away what was left of his wealth.

Shortly before she died, Grandmother Sophia van Dort sent for me. Alone, she lay. Marble-pale, against frilled lawn pillows, ice-blue eyes staring. "Kneel by my bed," she whispered. Trembling, I knelt.

Veined marble hands fumbled for the familiar white and gold-tooled Bible I had seen so often. "Take this in your hands, child. Now swear on this Bible that you will never drink, swear or smoke, nor let your mother or father do so."

I swore her oath, and it lay festering in my seven-year-old mind, breaking into hysteria at times.

One evening as my father sat in the garden smoking his cigar, a whisky and soda by his side; I ran and emptied the glass on the grass.

"Hey, Bunting, what the devil?" He asked angrily. My mother whispered to him.

"Oh my God!" he said. "This could be a problem!"

I remember going into a frenzy with my parents who were both reasonably sophisticated people, specially my father who smoked pipes or cigars when he had a little leisure-time, and drank one whisky every evening. My mother had started smoking after Yvonne's death. One tin of Gold Tipped cigarettes, a day.

❧

Gradually my mother began to return from the shadow land into which she had retreated. Her first attempt to return to normalcy began in the large poultry yard at the back. Every morning she went down to the chicken run to watch glossy Buff Orpingtons, Black Minorcas, and russet Rhode Island Reds run around. Then she'd search the egg hatches, very slowly. She let me collect a few eggs, still warm with the porcelain feel of them.

At home when my father had a spare moment he would corral my mother and me in his library and declaim heady poetry to us, throwing his arm wide, lowering his voice to a deep, theatrical tone that made me giggle. "Heathen!" my father would cry. "Listen to the music of this!" I teased him by looking blank, yet I could read the music of the words he spoke, and in a time ahead I would remember his analyses, explanations, the nuances of a particular passage.

During this uneasy time, with my mother still vulnerable, I did whatever I could to make her notice me. I ran in the rain, or fled next door over the wall to visit neighbours; I wrote a play of kings, queens, princes and princesses, in which the children next door took part, and persuaded my parents and their friends to see it acted "in aid of poor children".

I was sent to Bishop's College, whose grounds stretched to the shores of the Beira Lake. Its pupils travelled to school in rickshaws smelling of hot Rexene, watching the puller's whipcord muscles strain along his bare feet as they thudded on the road. Some arrived in a hackery cart, which seated four on narrow, facing seats, and was driven by a carter guiding an agreeable bull. For the rest, the new Fords now flooding the streets, with here and there some exotic car, high, with flopping, fold-back canvas hoods and polished brass headlamps.

Bishop's College was run by Anglican Nuns. Sister Eva, the Mother Superior, and Sister Mary, soft, dimpled. Under them was an assortment of excellent teachers. Here it was easier not to feel what I believed was my mother's rejection of me. I made new friends, cracked Ceylon Almonds that fell from the large-leafed *Kotang* trees. On Saturdays my friends and I had *spend-the-day* parties at each other's homes, played *Hide-and-Seek* over balconies and available rooftops, played fun cricket with the brothers, and watched them play serious cricket at inter school–matches, with sudden, new excitement.

Grandmother Spittel

My mother's indifferent correcting of me I ignored; my father's lazy, "Let her grow wild," was what I chose. Every Saturday I was sent to Weimar, to sit on the veranda steps and go over my tables with Aunt Agnes, who was sombre and regrettably plain. She walked up and down behind me brandishing a ruler, and setting sums. The time came when she commanded, "Now your thirteen times tables! Backwards!" I went on strike.

Immediately, Grandmother Spittel called from the veranda, "Stop persecuting the child, Agnes! Christine, come here!" She gave me some pumpkin preserve she had made with bees honey. As I scrunched into the crisp sugary coating, juice dribbled down the sides of my mouth and the scent of honey filled the air.

"Work hard," my little silver-haired grandmother whispered to the daughter of her favourite son when she kissed me goodbye. "Work harder," Aunt Agnes grunts. She was a good woman, and sincerely worried about my maths.

My father's obsession with learning had one advantage. Books he believed were the key to knowledge and they became my passion too. Books were to become for me the foundation of all I was to be; they were the panacea for my mother's grief, the storehouse of knowledge for my father's skills as a surgeon, writer, anthropologist, and lecturer.

But life had changed irrevocably. Now there were no more stories from my mother. When I asked her, tugged at her sleeve to make her listen to my frantic, "Mummy! Speak to me!" she looked at me vaguely and shook her head. Frightened, I escaped to William's garden, or next door, where the new-bride (not so new now) smiled and as always offered me fruit drinks. I climbed the *num-num tree* in the garden, but it was, somehow not high enough. Finally I invented a little sister called Frances with whom I had ephemeral dialogue.

One day my father overheard me, and crouched beside me, "Bunting, my dear child…who are you speaking to?"

"I'm lonely, Daddy."

He brought home from his jungles a Vedda child my own age to be my companion. Kaira. I can see him still: my father's shirt covering thin shoulders, the whites of his eyes like hard boiled eggs; the dark of his skin covered by the dirt of ages, for I learned later that they, the Vedda people, never bathed. Above all, I remember my mother crying out from her great silences, "Dick, this is a cruel thing you have done."

Kaira emerged from the house his head shaved, a make-do sarong and shirt far too large for his scraggy body, and stood there, mute, his hands hanging at his sides, his eyes like the eyes of a captured animal.

I approach on bare feet, sandals forgotten.

༄

My mother is restless. I can feel her restlessness though she does not move.

"Mummy?"

She does not answer. She speaks little since my baby sister died.

"Mummy! Speak to me!"

Still no answer.

Finally, "Ssh! Sleep! Close your eyes." But there were moving darks and lights thrown against the wall by the flickering kerosene night-lamp. I saw shadow dragons, movement, animal shapes more frightening than any sun-shadows.

My mother, a shawl thrown over her nightdress, went at last to sit quietly on the veranda. A dying moon would be shining too, on my father in a jungle alive with silently-moving animals. It is the first jungle trip he has made since they returned from England, torn apart, changed by the death of two-year-old Yvonne.

They are different. My mother cries or sits alone. My father works as if there is nothing else but his work. There is still *me*, I want to cry it out aloud to them. But I cannot speak to them. He is too busy. She does not hear me. I miss my mother who still grieves for her baby. Then… my mother is found unconscious, and it took time bringing her back. It is imperative we moved house – quickly.

❧

For my mother the annexe was drowned in memories of Yvonne and she would drown with them. A squat, ochre-coloured house in Ward Place, the Harley Street of Ceylon's doctors, was found for us. Meanwhile, from the shell of a two-storeyed annexe in its garden, was created Ceylon's first private Nursing Home. It had an operating table built in England to my father's specifications.

Immediately successful, it brought a new sense of drama with it. Something was always happening there, and I was, theoretically at least, involved in what was often a life and death struggle. So here I was, just eight, and I felt for the first time the throb of drama, of happenings of which previously I knew nothing about. Here Clarie, my mother, excellent physician that she was had her own part to play. Now, on an operating table tailored to accommodate his stiffened shoulder, my father performed major surgery, and as the doors of the operating theatre swung open, I'd get the odour of chloroform, surgical spirits, Lysol; I would catch a glimpse of a different father, capped, gowned and masked.

I became a precocious child too much for any ayah to handle. I was upgraded to having a proper English-speaking nanny. Poor Mary S. aged nineteen with a pale, pimpled face, and the most curious spoken English, became my long-suffering companion, alias nanny.

"Miss Christine, coming, going, running, jumping, reading under bed, climbing and reading on *Umbarella* tree branch, where cannot catch! What I do? She not doing what I tell, no? How can manage?"

I loved Mary. Once I locked her for fun in my parents' bathroom and forgot her. Two hours later my mother found her crying there, and was as angry as I had ever seen her. But when my father was told about it, though he gravely said, "Bunting, what is all this I hear?" I swear I saw the corner of his mouth twitch.

Yet my bond with Mary was strong, for she was essentially gentle. When she left to get married, I sobbed my heart out for I was lonely. Though I did not know it then, I would be, in a strange way, always lonely. Books continued to be, above all others, the single factor, the artery that pulsed through my life and gave me courage.

My mother had an over-protective relationship with me after the death of my sister Yvonne. She always made me carry a handkerchief pinned to my dress if I had a cold and stopped me playing normal games at school. She fussed and worried but was otherwise a wonderful, gentle mother.

My father felt corralled. Overloaded with work, needing more space, one day he exploded with the statement that he had found the land on which he would build his dream house and nursing home.

MY FATHER TOOK US one Sunday morning on a surprise drive. Past the neat suburban houses with their tailored lawns. Great trees lined every road in the island, probably flowering at the same time; bouquets of crimson, vermilion, pink; the houses lessening in number, now, cream-coloured, then petering out. He stopped at last in front of an empty road, with only the race track running away into the distance.

"We get out here," he said. Then spreading out his arms in front of him, "Here," he said.

I can still see that pool of water crusted with water lilies and jacanas - lily trotters - walking the lily pads; the kingfisher darting into the water for a fish from its perch on an overhanging branch of a scarlet-flowered flamboyant tree; the quiet land and all that greenness. There he built his house.

We called it Wycherley.

White egrets flew over the garden and nested in our trees. We had barbets, bablers plump as matrons hopping about in sevens. Birds of Paradise trailed ribbons of white or scarlet, kingfishers swooped, woodpeckers pecked happily at their favourite tree and made their nests. Tiny tailorbirds neatly sewed together sheltered leaves for nests, and laid strange and beautiful eggs of turquoise freckled with pale brown. Years later when I was writing regularly, a pair of tailor-birds stitched together the leaves of a grape-vine on the veranda by my study, and every day I waited for the fledglings to appear. One morning the nest was torn apart, the broken shells of the eggs scattered on the red cement floor. A year passed before they built another nest.

It was, I think, 1922 when Wycherley was completed. Nearly two years went in the building of it. From the first discovery of the land in an undeveloped part of Colombo, which would later become Colombo's prime residential area, the house grew steadily. Great pylons drove into the wet earth and emptied it, which saddened me for the birds, but there was excitement watching rooms grow. My father's consulting rooms, the large sitting and dining rooms with teak sprung floors. Then, the stairs. The first eight leading to a small landing; a few more to a larger landing; then the last fourteen; and the step that creaked when I crept too late upstairs after a dance. How strict my parents were to be about their only daughter.

The upper floor had wide corridors and many doors. My mother's 'Boudoir' as she called it, had pale blue walls and blue rose chintz covered chairs; her long- mirrored dressing table where she put up her hair with the silver-backed brush marked C.F. van D. At the end of the long passage, my father's library, lined with glass-fronted bookcases where he must have had a thousand books each allocated their own sections and guarded with DDT or naphthalene balls to keep damp and insects away.

His desk. A shadow man bends over it, writing. A shadow child asks, "Daddy, why are you always writing this rubbish. You are a doctor." The words return, echoing in a different age, "My dear child. Long after I am gone this will live on." Sometimes he would be seated in a cane chair with a plain rust cushion, creating in a black notebook his own sketches for some complex operation.

The day we moved in, our contractor hung mango leaves across the door for good luck, our architect insisted we cross the front verandah with our first steps facing West as the astrologers said we should for luck, carrying a bottle of milk for the boiling-of-the-milk ceremony done on the polished front verandah, where a small wood fire had been lit and rice cooked in milk until it frothed over. Then the architect, the contractor, my parents and I were offered trays of home-made sweetmeats for a happy homecoming.

If ever a house had a split personality, it was Wycherley - with its throbbing alter ego, the nursing home, separated from the main house by three steps upstairs, and downstairs by a passage from the consulting room.

Richard Spittel in front of Wycherley

Though my father quietly continued to perform innovative, brilliant surgery in his custom-designed operating theatre, with his carefully selected nurses, and was able to follow his cases through to successful conclusion, the nursing home brought an alien dimension into the main house.

Every morning my mother sat at the long dining table with a slate in front of her, giving orders to the cook who marketed for the day's supplies. Her theoretical knowledge of food was vast, though she did no cooking. Helped by *Mrs. Beeton's Cookbook* she could order anything from hospital diets to elaborate dinner menus, their preparation and presentation. Yet she hated to deal with food.

She was an intellectual, untidy, gentle, unpractical soul moulded uncomfortably into a different channel.

Secretly she must often have thought of the dreams she had had, the years spent in becoming a physician; or did she put those out of her mind? Occasionally when I sat on a small stool leaning against her knee as we relaxed in her boudoir, I would ask about those years, and her eyes would brighten as she told me about them. How, supported by her father, she had fought her mother's opposition to be a doctor. The years at Medical College followed by Edinburgh and Dublin. Then she would stop: her voice loses its melody, her eyes their sparkle, and I, a mother I wish I had known.

The extended nursing home ended any possibility my mother may have had for a less frenetic pace of life in Wycherley. But she was too deeply committed and it drained her.

Every day, when I glance across at Wycherley which lies across the lane, even though it is a school now, some new memory rises clear. Then I look away into the quiet curve of our crescent garden, a green cave sheltered by trees. Donald, our gardener is quietly, rhythmically sweeping away dead leaves. Overhead birds fly to their roosts; a tired moon fades into an unknown tomorrow.

"I, MISSEE. YOU, KAIRA. Yes?" My hand indicates all this. It is the language of story-books. The big eyes stare at me. Blank, uncomprehending.

Not till my parents had left the room did I succeed in teaching him anything. With a slate, pencil and picture books I started to teach him words. With a pointed finger first; then with a wooden frame threaded with beads on wires, I began to teach him numbers.

In time I taught him how to play hop scotch in the hot sand of our drive. "See," I say, demonstrating, on the sandy court I had sketched with a twig. "Like this." We climb trees; I, the low-hung *num-num* tree with fruit clinging like fat green toads to its trunk. He, by instinct, a high tree, monkey-fashion, and for the first time I get a glimpse of this aborigine child who has a picture memory of almost nude people, his people, climbing towering trees, and sheer rock faces for honey. It is a way of life with him.

For Kaira, the silence of the jungle was different from the uneasy dark of Colombo where wind blows sweet and dies to a whimper. There, one could watch leaves dance, hear a low sussurance above sound that comforted. In Colombo no one knew these secret things. They used what they called a match to produce fire, unlike the soft crack of strikalight and flint over flammable tree-bark cotton to make a fire. At night globes that hung from the ceiling burst into moons that made him shutter his eyes with a defensive arm.

In the jungle, he slept against the thin body of his mother under the moon and the stars in the angle of a tree spread with tender leaves, or under the dry grass thatch of a Vedda hut.

Kaira about 7 years old, 1919

Here, the darkness, dawn, light, they were all different. Even in the house there was too much to fear. The black object clamped like a giant spider on the wall, which from time to time abruptly screams like a devil and does not stop until the Big One speaks to it, then hangs it back on the wall.

But there was comfort in the familiar sight of peacock feathers in a jar, the skin of a spotted deer on the floor of the Big One's study and on which he'd have liked to sleep. Here he sometimes slept alone, or on a mat on a lonely cement passage. Curled up like an animal. Slowly he began to adapt himself, as memory began to fade.

Then one day in a corner of Sir's library he found the dried skin of a bear on the floor, glaring, teeth bared like that of the animal that had killed his mother - and ran screaming to the farthest corner he could find, crossed his skinny arms tightly about himself and let dry, harsh sobs, rack his body for the last time. After that, he did not cry whatever happened.

෨

The problem now was what to do with Kaira. No school would accept him. He was too estranged from his own people. I can see now that he was at that lonely age of adolescence when his future could lie anywhere, yet nowhere; and we were responsible, yet unable to know what thoughts roamed in that large head of his. On the carpet in the sitting room I started once again teaching Kaira his numbers, using my fingers, then a board stretched with wire and beads threaded on it; my scratchy old slate, and half of a slate pencil. We played dice, Snakes and Ladders, and he learned fast. Even smiled, when he won.

❧

But I had to go back to school. A new term had started and there was less time for Kaira. He grouched around while I was dropped at school, in my father's Ford car with the smelly carbide lamps, or with my ayah in a rickshaw with the remembered smell of hot red Rexene seats; watching thin legs pound red gravelled roads awash with fallen flowers gold, crimson, pink, from trees bordering the highways.

When I am at Bishop's College, I forget Kaira. For the first time now I had friends, I had fun; I ran after newly-hatched star tortoises on the shores of Beira Lake, climbed trees to collect emerald-green beetles; played hop scotch, ran races, *spent-the day* with friends on Saturdays, and dared to do, yet failed consistently in maths. But Kaira at home remembered his numbers. And when later, seated on the dining room carpet I taught him cards, he was better than I. Using the board strung with wires and coloured beads I taught him: "One! Kaira. Say one." –I flick it across and add another bead. "Two, Kaira. Two!" He cottons on to this game with astonishing speed. Quicker than I was doing at school.

❧

Yes, Kaira, jungle boy with a history of millenniums behind you, how would you settle into this family of two doctors torn apart by their grief for their second child? How would I, just started school at Bishop's College, help, or unaware, hurt you by teaching you to read and write a little English, and know your numbers.

Now almost alien in his white sarong and shirt, he was no longer the jungle child, but one on the verge of discovering, unknown to us, the harsh forest of a raw civilization beyond our house. The confining sarong now clamps his body, so he walks slightly splay-footed. The Sinhala tongue he is learning, instead of the staccato gutturals of the Veddas. He enjoys rice and curry, thrusting it with both hands into his mouth. Before, food had been hunted with bows and arrows; honey collected perilously, maize, irregularly planted, and boiled; his child-mother's breasts pummelled with both fists, to suck from her. Food was scarce. The memory of hunger slowly retreats; the present is ever-changing. The Lady was a sad, gentle person who seldom spoke. The Big Master, though thin as his own starved people, frightened him, yet he honoured him. He did not like being shown to the few, who were allowed to see him.

I did not like it either. My mother shrank back, then. Poor Mummy, who grew more distant, more silent in this house where her baby had been born.

᠅

Within me two creatures fought. The wild one and the tame one.

I wanted to grow wild but when I went with my mother to visit her dressmakers, the aristocratic German Misses von Possner, their hair in a fashionable pompadour, lace collars whale-boned to their throats, or go Christmas shopping to the Pettah, walking along covered pavements past shop fronts glowing with silks, toys, jewels, I was all hers. Here at Christmas-time my mother chose gifts for all my father's nephews and nieces. For me on Christmas Eve she secretly filled a pillow case with presents to hang at the foot of my bed.

My father took me to hospital with him to visit the children's ward to give them presents from my toys. I gave Kaira a new shirt, a pencil and note book.

Most of my friends have brothers or sisters, I wrote on the first page of a ruled exercise book I was given one Christmas as a diary. *But my little sister is gone.*

❧

As usual in the hot, dry season when the cicadas rasped, my father packed his jungle clothes and departed leaving no clue where exactly he was going, for he himself never knew.

Kaira showed no interest in returning to his jungles. It was difficult to know what his thoughts were as he helped a little about the house, and earned his first money. My parents worried about him. My father beginning to regret bringing this child of the forests to Colombo, grew irritable and worried about Kaira, making him impatient with the growing child, who in turn grew sullen.

When we moved to Wycherley, Kaira knew his letters. He could count. The games we had played, hop scotch, races, tree-climbing – could be played even better here than at the annexe, for there were many good trees to climb. I taught him more numbers. We played Snap. But soon I had less time to play with Kaira and then I had nothing more to teach him. There are days when Kaira hangs out in the background, sullen because I had little time to play with him. I was more interested in writing stories and plays.

But every now and then of an evening I would go to my swing in the back garden of Wycherley and he would push me. "Higher, Kaira! Higher!" I would cry, and laughing he would watch me jump at the highest point and pick myself off the grass. Then, even that stopped. Everything stopped. My parents stressed with selecting an English Public School for me, worried, and became more impatient with Kaira.

After I left for England I seldom forgot to write in my letters "How is Kaira?" and my father would answer, sometimes impatiently, sometimes with a chuckle; my mother seldom, but always with compassion.

❧

Nine years after he first came to us, Kaira ran away into the twilight of a nearby slum. No one could find him. He crept out of the passage where he slept, down the drive and out of the house over a barbed wire fence. It was the shortest way to where he was going. He passed people along the way who looked at him curiously, but he moved on, unconscious of their looks. There was one place, one place alone where he knew he would find shelter, where no one would harass him, no questions asked. Where he would be one of a group.

At last he found the shack along the banks of the canal. The stench was heavy, but he was not conscious of it. This perhaps, was the right door. Now he was less sure than he had been. There were so many 'entrances' - made of cardboard. Sacking. Bits and pieces of one thing or another. He knocked tentatively. Abuse was hurled at him. A toothless woman with a filthy rag thrown over her naked body yelled curses at him. He reeled back hurriedly. Two men locked in an embrace threw a quick look at him and laughed. Called after him, but he walked on.

"What are you doing here, you miserable ..." He walked past into an alley and turned quickly, hearing his name called. The twelve-year-old girl beckoned to him. "Come," she said.

Inside men sat playing with cards. He sat on his haunches and watched. Particularly the man who cheated. Yes, he could play like that, he knew. He waited his time until at last the head man jerked his head at Kaira. "You play?" Kaira nodded. The man invited him roughly to play, "You have money?" "Yes," and showed him twenty-eight rupees of the money he had stashed away. The watch he had stolen had fetched a good price. "Play, then." He had learned how they cheated too… But instinct warned him to lose a game or two, for safety.

The young girl watched him. There was something special she sensed about him. This boy had been hurt. Before dawn he returned to the big house as if he had never been away, this was the beginning. He came back for he had a hidden respect for the Big One, Lady, and Missee. But he knew where to go next time. And there would be no coming back then.

Through letters I learnt that all was not well at home with Kaira. They said he was getting plump and lazy; he was insolent to one of the nurses in the nursing home, who complained to my father. They said a watch another nurse had left on her dressing table by the window had gone missing. The next morning Kaira was gone. Caught a few days later, he was sentenced to three years at the Penitentiary.

That was the beginning. There were days when he would have liked to return to the big house; but then he remembered how he had been punished about the watch, and he shook his head.

SCATTERED ACROSS THE ISLAND at eleven-mile distances for coach-stops when the British first built their roads, were Government Rest Houses of identical plan, dissimilar only in size, in the more populated areas. No matter how remote, there was a reliable standard between them with identical Government stamped crockery, linen, service. When visitors arrived, a rest-house keeper hurriedly dressed in white, a tortoiseshell comb on top of well-oiled hair scraped back in a tiny knot at the nape of his neck would come running to meet them.

`"Coming, Sar, coming! What like for lunch, can giving curry-rice, sickin curry, rest-house pudding… Dinner, roast sickin, roast potato, beans, rest-house pudding… what like drinking now, Sar? Whisky soda got-it, beer, lime juice, lemnet." (Lemonade)

It was different at well-patronized Rest Houses on arterial roads spread like the veins of a hand along highways embowered in flower trees. But these were not the ones at which we stayed at, instead choosing the forgotten ones along minor roads with jungle environs, or a lonely sea or tank gemmed with water lilies, the haunt of wild birds and animals.

"Bunting, please don't run in the garden barefoot," my mother calls from the Rest House veranda. "Let the child run free!" snaps my father.

"She could pick up a germ from the garden, Dick. Get sunstroke."

Out of the corner of my eye, I see the two of them seated on the veranda, my father leaning back in his chair, wreathed in the smoke of a cigar, smiling slightly; my mother leaning forward. Brow furrowed.

"I found a feather!" I say, "and, see! A poor butterfly with a broken wing." Its amethyst wings cover the span of my hand.

"The purple Emperor." My father studies it. "This butterfly has scales that deflect light and gives it that metallic sheen. But look, the sheen is dulling as we watch, poor thing."

"Why do things have to die, Daddy?" I ask passionately.

"Cosmos. Look it up in the dictionary when you get back."

"But what happens afterwards?"

"Bunting, you'll tire Daddy with these questions. Anyway, lunch is ready." My mother's voice is gentle.

We sit down to a Rest House meal of country rice and a fiery curry from a chicken that had foraged the compound that morning. Later I follow my parents into the room with the mosquito-stained nets, the iron beds with coir fibre prickling through striped, ticking-covered mattresses, and Reckitts-blue-tinted sheets. My mother goes into the bathroom to cool her face with cologne and water and seconds later runs out, frantic. "There's a jumping frog on the wall by the mirror!"

"Better than a cobra or *polonga*," my father says placidly.

This is jungle country. My father's domain. After an afternoon siesta there is always an exploratory walk towards jungle or tank, to see what is 'out there.'

"Follow me closely," he says, loping ahead. Behind us a mother buffalo with a calf snorted furiously. My mother stands petrified between them. "For God's sake, Clarie! This way - quick!" Then, as she reaches us, and he steadies her, "What a damn silly thing to do, to get between a wild buffalo and her calf!"

She is silent all the way to Colombo, and I reach for her hand. She is so vulnerable, my mother. He, rigid now with remorse, but unable to find words to cancel what he has said.

When we returned to Colombo he made me go with him to buy her a piece of jewellery. "For scolding her. You choose it," he said, "I'm no good at this sort of thing." Together we selected a large, beautiful yellow sapphire teardrop on a platinum chain. "It's the colour of purest whisky," he said holding it up to the light. "You can't pay for hurts with presents," I said, surprising myself. He stared at me.

≈

"She adores you," said Reverend Waltham, who had long ago tutored him and was very old now, with a long white beard. "That, too, can be difficult. Dick, you always were inclined to be too impulsive in everything you did, everything you said."

"Who taught me Shakespeare's 'to thine own self be true'? I say what I think ..." he replies.

"There are ways of saying it," the old man said quietly. He leant on his stick to heave his great, black-clothed frame to its feet, and putting his hand on his pupil's shoulder said, "God be with you, my son." Bowing his head he was silent for a moment, then crossed himself. We did not know that we would never see him again.

≈

My father called me; he was studying with a magnifying glass a section of the island on the map before him.

"How would you like to sail to Wilpattu?" he asked amiably.

Our Game Sanctuary Wilpattu had no roads that led to its wild seacoast. That much I knew. "But you can't," I said.

"You can, my dear."

A Muslim patient had offered him one of his sailing boats, an Arab dhow, to travel the rare sea-route to Wilpattu, Ceylon's finest Game Sanctuary. Surprisingly, my mother, too said "Yes," for it was Christmas time. We would leave from Kalpitiya on the west coast of the island.

Against the sky of a hot December morning the mast of a strange sailing vessel rocked gently. Below the bow a carved floral panel carried in weathered white letters, *Mohideen Idroos*. For us, my father, mother and me, there was a palm-thatched cabin amidships lined with white calico where we arranged our camp beds.

A great barrel of fresh water was set by the mast; the boat was open to the elements in front, except at the extreme end, where a tiny cooking area was sheltered from the wind by a sacking curtain. Here, in the stench of bilge water and acrid smoke, a scraggy twelve-year-old Moorish boy, Haniffa, cooked, punctuating his work with heavy breathing and sniffs. Summoned, he would creep out of his lair with chilli-reddened eyes, and with a hitch at his sarong, turn his hand to whatever he was asked to do.

As we sailed into the evening, the captain, the tyndal, brought us to anchor in the calm waters of a river mouth. A jungle moon had risen and hung pallid in the sky. Against it our boat rocked gently, its mast pointing towards the stars. All night the vessel sailed in the pathway of the moon.

We were never out of sight of land: on one side, the mainland coast, on the other, like strands of seaweed, green islands. Beyond lay the haunted pearl banks destroyed by dredgers.

We camped in an empty palm-thatched hut near the fishermen's encampment. Behind, the land sloped towards the dense jungles of the Reserve.

We were setting up camp when a devil wasp stung my lip. By evening my face had ballooned and I developed a rising fever. Next morning it continued to rise. As from a great distance away, I heard my father say, "I'll have to… Can't risk encephalitis…" But I was past caring what he intended to do. Vaguely I remember my mother holding my head steady against her lap. Her quiet voice saying, "Bunting, drink this," holding neat brandy to my lips. Then covering my eyes with a folded handkerchief, she held my shoulders steady as my father's gloved hand made a lightning nick with his scalpel.

The fishermen brought gifts of fresh-caught fish. Haniffa grilled these on an open fire with smoke curling into the flavour. They brought prawns with the taste of the sea for my parents. For me, herbs my father asked them to find in the jungle, some as a healing salve for my fast-healing lip, some as a broth, for he knew of the secrets of ayurveda. Next day I was almost well.

At midnight, incredibly, we woke to the wind-blown sound of a church bell, for this was Christmas Eve, and the tiny Catholic church of the fishermen lay a quarter of a mile away.

The approach to the church was decked with wild-flowers: jasmine and white bryony; a crimson flowering creeper threading branches of a yellow-flowered shrub; the flame of Gloriosa Superba, against smoky plumes of grass; convolvulus and wild-pea veining the sand with amethyst. Overhead, a Fish Eagle soared, its wings motionless, until it dived swiftly into the sea and up again with a fish and flew away.

Beyond, sheltered by thick undergrowth and guarded by a barrier that kept wild animals out, we found the church of the fisher-folk and saw through the gloaming of pale candlelight the framed face of the Virgin above a tiny altar. Loving hands had laid the red brick floor; extra care must have gone into the plaiting of the coconut leaves that formed its roof and walls. I stood in a prayer that had no words and found my parent's arms round my shoulders.

In the two days that followed, my father, mother and I walked slowly along the beach, and spoke of many things. We spoke of stars, and other moons; of prehistoric creatures, and this island.

And how in ancient days, elephants roamed the hills in their thousands, and mermaids were thought by mariners to live in these seas, called the Mermaid Coast, but they were huge, pallid mammatees or dugongs who harmlessly swam these waters, and breast-fed their young.

During those days how close the three of us were. It was good to talk together, totally free, as perhaps we never had before. At dawn my father walked his jungles (although against the rules) with one of the fishermen and returned, for breakfast on the beach, his eyes shining.

He'd sighted the largest herd of spotted deer he'd ever seen, many elephants, a leopard up a tree, a python… each with some added gem of information. On that last evening as the three of us sat quietly on the beach watching the sun go down, he said, "We are the privileged ones who can still find places little changed by man. How long will it last? Not even your lifetime, Bunting."

I knew with sudden clarity that there would never come again such closeness between the three of us.

છ

At Easter, when the heat seemed to bore into every layer of our skins, my mother and I went to the hills of Nuwara Eliya for the tennis championships, the Races, and the Season for which everybody, except my father, went. Instead, this was his season to locate every true Vedda in the country, and to tell the truth I would rather have gone with him.

We stayed with two friends of my mother's who lived not far from the tennis courts where all Colombo society gathered to watch the greatest tennis tournament of the year. It was my mother's happiest time, for the heat of Colombo destroyed her. Here she laughed often, and there was more than a shadow of the beautiful young woman she had been.

'Aunt' Minnie and 'Aunt' Molly (everyone over thirty automatically became Aunties) stood at the honeysuckle-draped front door to meet us. "Darlings!" they cried in unison, Aunt Minnie tremolo, Aunt Molly alto, "How simply lovely to see you again!"

"And Christine, goodness how she's grown!" cried Aunt Minnie who was as thin as her sister was rounded. "What is she now? Nine?"

"Eleven, nearly twelve."

"Clarie dear, don't you think she's a bit, well, thin, for her age? I mean…"

"Molly doesn't mean it badly, dear, do you dear?"

"No of course not," they warbled together. "After all, dear, you are a doctor, and very brave of you, too, I mean all the horrid illnesses around."

"Be quiet, Minnie," hissed Aunt Molly.

"We dine at eight," trilled Aunt Minnie as we went to our rooms.

My mother touched an immaculately laid bed with hand-embroidered sheets. "They're really very sweet," she said.

❧

Up the hill from us were the spreading grounds of close friends with a large joyous family. Every one was welcome there. Friends, friends of friends, any stranger who cared to drop in could be seated at their vast dining table, which could take a dozen and a half people, and if there were more, it was no problem.

They were a sporty family. Gil, the only daughter, was a school friend; suddenly I found myself a little shy with the boys. Any boy. It was peculiar.

We watched the tennis finals; and the Gold Cup races where the same owner, whose horses always won, won again, but I persuaded my mother, who preferred predictable things, to bet on the horse whose jockey wore the nicest colours. It came last.

I climbed Mount Pedro as we called Pidurutalagala, with our gang, went on drives away and over the hills, on a picnic, to a tea estate, anywhere... The hills were blue, the pine trees sweetly scented, and one was young and free in a way that would never come again, though I did not know it. Soon afterwards, everything changed.

I was to go to school in England. By ship. To be left there. Never to come home for holidays.

WE SAILED FROM CEYLON with enormous cabin trunks on a ship called the *Oldenbahnveldt*. As the ship's engines began to purr, my father lay prone on his bunk, stretched his knobbly hands neatly at his sides, and closed his eyes.

This was his ploy ever since he first boarded a ship as a young doctor setting out for his further degrees and was terribly seasick. This (he said) was the best way of dealing with his sea-sickness. It saved a great deal of trouble later. I was distressed. Mummy took me by the hand and led me out on deck to see our island slowly disappearing.

I have blurred memories of what my feelings were. Excitement predominant, but with it, churned-up feelings that made me clutch my mother's hand and say, "Please, Mummy, I feel seasick too." She pointed at seagulls and told me a story about them.

It was an exciting voyage. When my father recovered he told me sea-stories, pointed out dolphins following the ship, told me about the great albatross of other seas. Our closest friend was a tall, wistful Englishman who loved Ceylon, and was leaving it for good. His name was John Still.

There was the excitement of going through the Suez Canal, stopping at Port Said. Camels, minarets, palm trees. Arab traders swarming aboard to sell the silks of Arabia, flinging across the deck an extravaganza of crimson, gold and peacock silks. Shawls embroidered in sprays of rainbow colours. An Arab spread one over my knobbly shoulders, and for the first time a strange thrill shuddered through my body; my shoulders straightened, instinctively I threw a corner across a shoulder, let it fall close, and wrapped in this new sensation felt my whole body tingling, aware... Aware of what? "If you were three years older, my dear," said John Still, quite seriously, "I would buy it for you." Three years seemed a long time to wait. To wait for what?

☙

We landed at Marseilles. I remember cobbled streets but were there really that many in 1926? Was the hotel really *the* Hotel Normandie? Here was a crowded foyer, a lift one worked oneself with an open-grill door through which you could see where you had been and where you were going. I tried it once alone; it started valiantly, but halfway between the first and the ground floor stopped. There, like a caged creature I stood, I could see people staring at me, I stared back, incoherent. M. Julien who had taught me his Mauritian French had not taught me how to call for help. Eventually I was rescued and marched ignominiously to my parents' room.

But even here was something new to explore. Behind a discreet pink screen I saw a dumpy, white basin-like affair with taps marked *chaud* and *froid*, which even I knew from M. Julien's coaching meant hot and cold. Experimentally I turned them on. Immediately fountains of water cascaded over me, the good French carpets, everywhere. Shrieks from my parents followed by bells ringing furiously for a maid, who muttered in French as she mopped, and who departed, still muttering, despite her generous tip.

My father impatiently sent Mummy and me out to shop at a *Magasin* department store while he talked with the French driver, Robert Chavasse, who was to drive the car my father had bought in France on that last disastrous visit with my mother six years ago.

We returned to find him with a highly distressed Robert, who, dressed in a smart uniform and well-polished boots looked more like a distinguished soldier than a chauffeur.

"But your car, it is very old, M'sieu," Robert was saying.

"Nonsense," my father replied crossly. "So, tomorrow morning at nine, then…"

❧

"*Vous êtes noir,*" the little French maid in Paris said eyeing me with curiosity as she brought in my tray of supper while my parents were at the Folies. "*Je n'est pas noir,*" I replied with dignity. "*Je suis brun.*" "*Je ne comprends pas, chérie,*" she answered. Shaking her head and smiling as she flounced back with the tray. My parents returned from the Folies, my father pleased with his evening, my mother strained. "It was beautiful," he said when I awoke. "Why couldn't you take me?" I complained.

They looked at each other. "Later," they said in unison. Five years later I did go and was moved by its beauty and the beauty of other places - Italy… Venice, the gondoliers, the flowers; Austria, Germany, Paris, the palaces of Versailles and Fontainbleu, the museums, art galleries.

Later we visited Holland and saw the famous picture of *The Night Watchman* my father had told me so much about. But it had been cleaned, and now no longer *The Night Watchman* the painting we looked at showed a different, less intriguing dawn scene. In Scotland, years later, I would see a picture of the Virgin and Child which needed cleaning and as they cleaned the Child disappeared and the face of the Virgin changed, it was the face of Mary Magdalene.

❧

We said goodbye to our charming Robert Chevasse and the AA driver Smith took his place. Through England, Scotland, Wales he drove us stiffly, obviously disapproving of and unused to unusual characters like us. Uncaring, blithely, my father kept up his mission of *educating Christine,* interspersing his act with poetry. In Wales there was still one lonely village in the craggy hills where they wore tall-pointed witches' hats, and stared as we passed. Here too, deep gorges plunged into crevasses far below. In Scotland we saw lochs, heather-hills and wild blueberries to gather by the handful. In London we visited the British museum; the Geographic museum and saw a giant skeleton of some beast that had lived a millennium ago.

And with all this store of knowledge behind me, I went to school where my history, geography, and the rest were taught on a more solid foundation than I ever had.

I WAS A CHILD of twelve when I went to my boarding school in England; a naive eighteen when I returned home six years later. Ships still took three weeks to travel across the seas.

Small, scraggy, scared, I crouched in the front seat of the bus that took us from Brighton Station to Roedean. As its doors swung open before what was to be my house for the next six years, I found myself sprawled gracelessly onto the grass verge.

Crisp English voices asked "You all right?"

"Yes, thank you."

They walked into the house chattering. I dusted myself off and followed.

"So you come from Ceylon," said Miss Ford, kindly. Some instinct told me that the elegant, silver-haired Miss Ford, my housemistress, had already assessed me as a problem child.

It was an understanding school for they wrote with solicitude in my reports that "Christine is doing well, but she is always looking out of the window." Yes, past the grey gulls calling over the grey ocean, and beyond to a turquoise sea.

It was a disciplined school, and I had come from home where I ran free. But after a while, one grew a skin of acceptance, and then, of immense pride at being there.

"You speak English well," the fifteen-year-old sub-prefect ordered to take me round the grounds said.

"I don't speak anything else."

"This is the gym," she said, disconcerted, and I trotted after her through swing doors opening into what seemed to me an arena. But everything was fine after that, except that I kept looking beyond the circling gulls, not knowing that I was doing so.

The first three terms went well (except for arithmetic).

In the fourth term I woke covered with spots. Within minutes I was bundled into a small pony cart with Miss Ford and trotted to the sanatorium at the other end of the grounds to share a room with two other girls with measles.

On the third day I woke with an earache and could not hear. A specialist from town operated on my ears. Then I started to die of something else with baffling temperatures soaring from 105 degrees to subnormal, and back again. My mother who had stayed back until I was settled had been getting ready to leave. She cancelled her passage back to Ceylon, and sat by me. I did not know her or any of the white-gowned people who drifted in and out of the sterile room. But I remember once clearly seeing a small girl on a bed below me, before drifting back into nothingness.

In Ceylon my father was going berserk with the urgent daily cables sent him.

Then one morning, I stirred, and a gentle hand touched mine. "Bunting…"

"Mummy?"

It took a long time to get strong enough to return to school. On the doctors' advice my poor mother took me to Switzerland to 'get strong again.' But when I returned to school I had missed a vital one and a half terms and never caught up.

A holiday home was found for me at a Rectory in Yorkshire. The Vicar and his wife who were to be my guardians were the parents of our Vicar in Colombo.

❧

Years later driving across the Yorkshire moors with Alistair my husband, I saw a small signboard pointing up a village road.

The Vicarage still stood there, a gaunt early 18th century house next to a small church. Looking onto the road was the narrow rectangular window of the room where I had spent my holidays.

⌘

Violet Ricketts, the daughter, met my train at York. Tall, full-breasted, almost sixty, with a high country flush and a mass of straw-coloured hair, she slowly, silently, looking neither to right nor left, drove me across the lonely West Riding of Yorkshire.

The Reverend and Mrs. Ricketts, like their daughter Violet, matched the Rectory. He was 84, she perhaps 75, and Violet passing 50. Mr. Ricketts, white haired, pink cheeked, appeared at meals and disappeared for the rest of the time, except when he took the service at the tiny church next door. Mrs. R., still beautiful, was haughty. Violet... Ah, Violet, who wore her faded blond hair in a pompadour was given to singing hymns in a piercing contralto. At the rectory, she sang away, breaking fiercely at times into *Green-sleeves*. They were good people, doing good and charitable things. Like accepting the awful responsibility of taking a cinnamon-coloured child during the holidays.

I walk to the village along an empty road with hedgerows thick with blackberries, past an empty cart, a shaggy-footed horse grazing. The village is a cluster of cut-stone cottages with picture-postcard gardens and in the centre a post office. I buy stamps and black and white peppermints, and think suddenly, sharply of my parents.

Returning I stop at the church. It has a gentle quietness with its slumbering memorial tablets and embossed coats of arms. I kneel for a moment in a back pew, squeezing my eyes against sudden homesick tears.

In the graveyard someone has placed a jam jar of fresh chrysanthemums against a dying bouquet of roses, and I wonder who were the people who lived here long ago. This is Jane Eyre country: the book I have just finished for holiday reading.

Darling Mummy and Daddy,

The first summer hols! I'm sitting in the garden under an enormous copper beech. This garden is full of trees, lovely herbaceous borders and a lawn stretching to gorse-covered moors where two chestnut coloured horses graze.

Every morning at eight we all troop into the study for prayers. Mrs. R., Violet, me, then the Cook and the three maids in starched caps and aprons.

We use lamps and candles here. It's creepy going upstairs to bed with a small lamp or a flickering candle, and as I pass the landing-window I can see the graveyard. My room is very cold though it's summer. Last night I was reading in bed by the light of three candles, and Mrs. R. came in and said, "What! Three candles!" And blew one out. It was really weird. But don't worry, I'm fine.

The food is super! Homemade bread of every kind baked twice a week and the whole house smells of baking. (Everything comes from the garden or nearby farms.) Mr. R. carves the Sunday Roasts and they are fabulous. He is rather sweet, but VERY old. Daddy, at table he told me he'd read your book, "Wild Ceylon," and he thought it "Interesting, of course rather simply written." I am still absolutely FURIOUS!!! It's a LOVELY book! I'm still angry.

All my love,
Me

Another term passed and another.

Darling M & D,

The grass has a crusty film of ice and it's REALLY freezing. I'm wearing two pullovers. It's a lonely house few visitors visit. 'They' don't visit much either, except Mr. R. who does parish things. There's church twice on Sundays, and even when there's no one but us, Mr. Ricketts gives 'a short address', and Violet sings away in a sad, shrill voice. I read a lot, and sketch. There was only us in church this evening.

How COULD you both agree with Mrs. R's suggestion that I should be coached in arithmetic here, of all places! I have to walk about half a mile through a wood to get to Miss Perkins, who's ancient. It gets dark early, and when I return the wind wails, and the branches thrash like witches' arms towards me. I was upset today. Mrs. R. asked me something and I shrugged, as we all do in Ceylon. Mrs. R. whipped round and hissed, "How DARE you shrug your shoulders when I speak to you!" Oh well, don't worry. I've stuck it out for two hols, and it really does get better. Next hols: Spring! And then I'll be sixteen and you two will be here for the summer hols. HOW SUPER!

P.S Violet drove me to Malton to order my new suit from the tailor who makes outfits for the Hunt people. A tiny shop, two steps down into a dark room full of bales of cloth and musty with the smell of wool, and the fitter running round me with a bit of chalk. The beautifully tailored suit of fine navy-blue herringbone wool makes me look different.

All my love,
Me

Then spring came to West Yorkshire.

I walked in the woods to day. The leaves were bud-green, and all the ground was covered with bluebells and daffodils, and down by the stream lily-of-the-valley grew wild. The village children were gathering armfuls of flowers and we were all so happy. But when I returned Mrs.R. was furious and said I was never to do so again. But I loved it, and I loved them. WHY was it wrong? Daddy, please explain this to me with your special understanding of simple people. You would have been glad for me, wouldn't you, both of you?

I have a strange feeling that one-day all this will go; the flowers, the children playing in the woods and differences between people. Maybe there'll be no wild flowers in the woods, and children, different. It will all be different. But 'just now' I will always remember. I long to see you both again. There is so much I don't understand. Who am I? What am I? Brought up here to be, to think, English; yet WHAT?

P.S. Next time, July. London!

The summer holidays in London, then in Kandersteg with my parents were a disaster. From the day we met I was startled at the sight of my father. I'd let him grow in my memories into something different. Now he seemed small, almost quaint with his quirky smile, and his flat accent. Idiosyncrasies I had loved in Ceylon suddenly seemed appalling in the sophisticated climate of London. And seeing this, he accentuated them, noisily stirred his coffee at breakfast in both directions until people stared, and I whispered, "Daddy! Don't! Please!" From that day on, it was war, undeclared and horrible. Between us my mother hovered distressed, able to see both points of view.

He left earlier than he intended, and as we stood on the station platform, I put my arms round him. "Daddy, I'm sorry. So very sorry."

He answered quietly. "I came all this way to see Bunting; and all I could find was a stranger. Don't get lost," he said.

☙

They made different holiday arrangements for my last two terms.

'Aunt' Lucie van Langenberg, a close friend from Ceylon who lived with her doctor son in Bedfordshire, was a delightful change. Silver-haired, with a twinkle in her eyes and a wonderful sense of humour, I adored her. She introduced me again to an island I had almost forgotten, for her background there went far into the time of the Dutch East India Company from which my own parents were descended.

Seated in an over-stuffed armchair in front of the fire with me on the carpet at her feet, she would tell me of her Ceylon, of long ago.

If I had asked her about sex she would have been my wisest teacher, for I was curiously innocent. My mother had totally avoided the subject, which she kept saying I would find out at the right time. Aunt Lucie's stories, full of fun and forgotten scandals set me wondering.

"Aunt Lucie!"

"It's true! Would you like a chocolate?"

Words tripping over each other, eyes bright, she'd describe vast family gatherings in Ceylon at Christmas and Easter. "Everyone had enormous families, my dear, - at least ten or twelve children, all the grand-children, cousins, unmarried aunts and lonely people. Tables groaning with silver dishes of turkey, a huge ham, crackers, Dutch Breudhers and a round, red ball of Dutch Edam cheese, with butter set on ice to stop it from melting. And small, select dinner parties, the gentlemen sitting over their brandy and cigars, after the ladies had left for the drawing-room to talk about the latest scandal."

Had change reached my island yet, or would the people I had known remain engulfed in a world of another era? Would there be enormous changes in the time to come?

I felt scared, then. How would I fit in? A child-woman vaguely aware that she might belong to disparate cultures; wildly romantic, but totally unaware of sex, except that 'it' happened.

Every now and then Aunt Lucy would suggest we went up to London to shop. She would put on her smartest red couture suit, red high-heeled shoes, her (real) pearls, and a little lipstick - for me, too, and we'd trot off happily. She bought me my first high-heeled shoes, took me to get my hair done, Scrutinized me and said, "For goodness sake when you return take off those glasses in public at least! You'll manage." Then, her head on a side, her eyes bright as a bird's, "You could look quite reasonable if someone took you in hand."

"You, Aunt Lucy?"

"Mmm." she said, looked at me again, and hugged me. "I would have loved to, darling," she said.

1931-1933

All Grown Up

To me, being grown-up meant smoking cigarettes, drinking cocktails, and dressing up in high heels and glamourous outfits.
- Lorna Luft -

I WAS EIGHTEEN WHEN I returned to Ceylon.

Wycherley still stood alone, with the long fields of amber and green grassland behind, and on the right, the Government-reserved land of the Irrigation Department, with a skin of water, and jacanas as before, delicately treading lily pads. From the front balcony, the racecourse stood clear and on Saturday afternoons horses galloped past. Finally we went, my mother, father and I, to stand on the balcony of my room. The busy graphite mine with bare-bodied men returning from work in skins of pewter had gone; instead virgin land stretched past blurred trees and the shaggy heads of palms to the lovely, amethyst outline of Adam's Peak, and Wycherley was islanded in green.

On that first day back in Colombo, in the flurry of seeing my father again, the excitement of the staff lined up on the veranda of Wycherley to meet "little Missee." The phone rang – for me. I recognized the voice of someone I had known in Ceylon when we were both children, and had met once in London with my mother. "Welcome back," he said. "Come with me to a Boxing Day dance this evening." Before I could answer he said, "I'll call for you at eight."

The designer dress from London made me look different. Mama's pearls softened the collarbones I hated. I peered at my reflection, added a flick of colour on my cheeks, an inexpert dash of eye-shadow and immediately removed both. Downstairs a bell rang. I panicked.

My parents stood in the doorway.

My mother said, "Lovely, darling."

My father shook his head slightly. "How young..."

I stood up sweeping a brush off the table. "I don't want to go to this dance! I don't know anyone! I'm not going!"

"Snap out of it, Bunting!" My father said quietly.

I stood glancing like a frightened animal from my mother to my father. Then I ran to my father, as I had done when I was a child, put my head on his shoulder and wept. It was over in a minute.

The bell downstairs rang again.

My mother said, "The present, Dick." My father held out a small box, "From Mummy and me, to welcome you home." Inside was a small pair of eardrops; the tear-shaped moonshine pearls came from Ceylon's vanishing pearl banks.

My mood swung as I ran downstairs for my first date. Guy - good looking, sophisticated, only a few years older than I - was waiting.

~

The friends I had known had grown into elegant young people, who danced superbly. I missed steps, murmuring "sorry" until my partner, a man older than most of the others said, smiling, "You shouldn't apologize, you know. They were all wondering what you would be like."

"Why?"

"Poor little Rich Girl, the famous surgeon's daughter."

I pushed away from him and hurrying into a room off the dance floor leant against a table. Overhead fans moved sluggishly; waiters in white shirts and sarongs slid past with trays of drinks. My hand, moving restlessly against the polished grain of the table caught a snag and snatching my hand away I saw a splinter, a drop of blood.

Rich girl? We never talked money in our home. My parents lived quietly, and Wycherley was a house of healing where books and learning, not things or wealth, had priority. It was strange to return and find myself a stranger.

"You look as if you could do with a drink,"

I had not noticed the man who now stood near me. Without waiting for a reply he beckoned to a passing waiter and handed me a glass.

"Something wrong?"

"Nothing!"

"Sure?"

"Only that I've just come back home after six years away, and feel a stranger."

"Just watch out for the pack that'll hover round. Your father told me you'd been away a long time. He was worried how you'd adjust."

I edged back onto the table, studying him. Though he wore the dog collar of a priest, his black, short-sleeved shirt and brown trousers were informal. I glanced again at the dog collar, and the cinnamon brown face above it.

"You know my father?"

"Who doesn't?"

"I didn't know he was that famous."

"You've been away a long time," His voice was kind, so kind that I burst out, "I don't know how to deal with all this! I've never been to a dance before, except once with my mother and father."

He laughed, and I started to laugh, too.

"That's better. The child has a sense of humour."

"I'm not a child. I don't even know your name."

"We'll meet again. I have to go, now."

"With no other advice for the Poor Little Rich Girl?"

"Learn how to dance," he said, smiling. Then his smile switched off. "Learn to laugh at yourself, too. Rule three: Don't marry the first man who asks you. Rule four: It won't do you any harm to break some of the shibboleths of your public school. Have you forgotten, or perhaps you have never known, what it is to run free like an animal in your father's jungles? The responsibility is yours. Enjoy life! So, until we meet again, child-woman."

❧

The 30's and 40's were a wonderful time for the small community of Dutch Burghers – that small remnant of people, of whom I was one, whose ancestors had come when the Dutch invaded and took the island of Zeilan in the seventeenth century. With their knowledge of Roman script they were quick to adapt to the mandatory written and spoken English, and rose rapidly in their professions.

My grandfather van Dort, travelling in a sailing ship that left from Galle Harbour, furnished his cabin with a pewter ewer and basin, and a trunk-full of books to study on the three-to four-month voyage via The Cape. At times the great sails billowed, and the vessel rode the high waves fast; but in the doldrums when they hung limp, passengers grew sick of the sight of each other's faces, and physically sick as fresh rations dwindled, and salt beef took the place of fresh chicken or goat, and the cow went dry, and had to be slaughtered. The next generation, my mother's, traveled by steam ships, via the newly opened Suez Canal, but still from Galle's rocky harbour, soon to be abandoned for steamers. And I, the third generation, sailed from Colombo's new harbour, and returned to find the brothers of my friends had become the bright young professionals of their day. The girls, bright, restless, talented; crazy about clothes; dancing to gramophone music at each other's homes; private fancy dress parties and very correct birthday balls. In the background, among the men there was a deepening interest in Communism.

The day I arrived my old school friend Millicent had the Wedding of the Year with a thousand guests. She was eighteen. I, also eighteen, had not even been to a dance, nor during the time I was in England even met any boys.

Another friend, Isolde, had just become engaged, her clothes were fabulous. Her jewellery matched what she wore, and a top tailor more or less lived at their house in Colombo, where under her mother's scrutiny he pinned, fitted and produced model outfits. On one occasion he was sent four times to the cinema to study a black velvet dress of Greta Garbo's that he copied minutely. At her 21st Party, the large central area upstairs was converted into a ballroom, and Isolde stood, slender, cool as a reed in the white dress her mother had ordered from Chanel. Later, her dark hair immaculate, she danced, her face showing no emotion; round her throat emeralds and diamonds her father had given her with earrings and a bracelet to match. Many years later in London I was asked by Isolde, then married and separated, to dinner at her flat. There, abruptly taken ill, she disappeared while we - Alistair, an Indian princess, a Yugoslav prince, and a friend sat talking until we were summoned, *sans* our hostess, to dinner. During coffee the Prince disappeared and presently returned with a bundled handkerchief in his hand. Turning aside, he opened it to show the contents to his friend, and I saw the gleam of emeralds and diamonds. I never saw Isolde again, nor knew what became of the wealth her parents had left her.

My own life back in the island was a strange mixture of control and freedom – up to a point – and when I returned, my mother insisted that it was etiquette for the two of us to 'call' on her friends, more or less to present me to them. I forget the ritual, which seemed to me crazy, but we had elegant cards, with our names inscribed in spidery copperplate, with the right top corner of one turned down for some obscure reason, were left at the gate. It meant, I believe that I was ready to be introduced to society. Or, that I was back in the island and available. Horrible thought! Our call was promptly followed by an invitation to take tea at each other's houses.

There I sat erect, hands crossed on my lap, following this pretence in this little England in Ceylon of the silver tea services, erect backs, dulcet toned conversation about trivialities, delicate little asparagus sandwiches, tea and small talk to wash it down.

I raged at my father. "Why do I have to go, too? This is home."

"Home is a strange mixture of behaviour, my dear. Your mother conforms to the British way in which she was brought up. Go if it pleases her."

"And you?"

He eyed me over the rim of his whisky and soda. "What do you think?"

≈

Christine and Prince at Wycherley, 1933

There was much to learn, maybe to unlearn. To meet life, not hide from it. To adjust to a different kind of people who were my people. But my thinking had changed; my speech made me a stranger to my own people – until they grew used to it. They had grown up, boys and girls together, playing then, for fun; playing now for serious. While I, untouched by emotion, felt only the 'romance' of it, as if, at twelve, when I was taken to school, emotion had frozen. It was a problem my father realized sooner than my mother.

"She'll grow out of it," was how they approached it, for they had grown distanced from emotional conversation.

They were undoubtedly disappointed that I had not made university. Every letter they wrote contained some gem of advice on the learning process. "You have inherited my bad memory," wrote my father. "The only way I can remember is to write it down, and keep coming back to it repeatedly in your mind whenever you can." In every one he enclosed funny cuttings from the newspapers; told of happenings in the General Hospital or in his nursing home – brought in a bit of scholarship – a line from the Greeks, the music of a poet. An enormous Webster's Dictionary lay open on a wooden stand in his library for easy reference; there were beautifully illustrated books on the lives of great artists, musicians… But I had indeed inherited his bad memory and in no way became a scholar.

At first, adaptation to island life was a thing of the senses. I loved the sensuous scent of the crimson and white frangipani that laid their petals like confetti on the red gravel of our drive. In the morning I heard the scratch of the gardener's ekel broom rake as he swept the flowers away. Still they bloomed, fell and bloomed again, scratching at senses not fully awakened. The parched smell of dust that powdered the tops of cars and the surfaces of old, polished wood at Wycherley; the hot, smarting, remembered smell of curry, coriander, cumin, chilli; the damp, crumbly feel of books in my father's library, the mustiness of cupboards.

I wandered through the house, searching for its voice. Not the remembered voice of the child who had run barefoot and slid down banisters; the child who had *spend-the-day* parties with her friends, and unknown to parents played hide-and-seek over balconies and on roofs; the child who was swung long ago by a Vedda boy called Kaira on the back lawn, and when it was at its highest jumped laughing onto the grass.

What happened to Kaira, Daddy?

He ran away, Bunting.

But why?

Civilization was too much for him. He became involved with an underground group, went to prison and disappeared. He died of syphilis, they said.

I went away and wept.

❧

Two days later I was being driven past the Eye Hospital when I saw among the crowd crossing the road a man with eyes like hard boiled eggs. "That Kaira, Missee," said the driver. I looked back but he had melted into the crowd.

❧

I had to get used to having my hair done while I sat snared like a bird in curtained cubicles. I sat through my parents' formal dinner parties. Crystal and polished silver accents, except for my father's dry, proud Ceylon accent. My own accent, polished and silvered in England produced platitudes. These were my first formal dinner parties.

On my eighteenth birthday when I was still in London before returning home, my father gave me a car – a Wolseley Hornet Special. I called her Fifinella, for she was bonny in her coat of green and silver and promised to fly with the wind. With the car went the premise that I would learn, not only to drive it, but also to look after it at a school of motoring in London.

The maintenance teacher was young and good-looking with black, sleeked-back hair and eyes that looked deeply into mine as he spoke of things of which I had absolutely no knowledge and probably would never need to know. How to change a wheel, how to investigate trouble under the bonnet I could not even open.

All the time his voice told me all I needed to know according to the rules, it washed over my head, and I doubt if he had ever had a more stupid pupil. However, they gave me a certificate stating I had received tuition.

Driving was another matter. My second tutor suggested we hire a lockup garage in a quiet suburb, from where he could give me practice lessons in driving on quiet roads, and I did well enough to get the same sort of certificate I'd had before, with which we returned with Fifi to Ceylon.

It was only there that, unknown to my father I really learned to drive.

Here, Fifi came to life, her engine purring as I put my foot on the accelerator and let the wind blow my hair. I was taught the racing change of the 1930's: 'stamp on the accelerator between changing gears.' Took crazy chances, for suddenly I had become self-conscious about the glasses that had made me look like an owl during those frustrating years behind me. In the three months I had had with my mother in London before we returned, my eye surgeon had suggested, "You're eighteen now; on the edge of life. Forget your glasses; wear them only when really necessary, at the theatre, cinema." Sometimes when I was driving I forgot to wear them…

I loved driving. With the hood back, the little green and silver car came alive. Now she was a mermaid swimming with the tide of traffic; now a creature of its own, daring me to overtake a lorry while another car approached. Twice there were accidents, a small one, and one bigger.

One day I had for the first time to appear in Court for a driving fault. At the end the judge had said, with a hint of smile "I understand you are the daughter of Dr. R.L. Spittel. I would have thought his daughter would have more sense of responsibility than you have shown. You are dismissed, but don't do it again." and there was a titter around the courtroom.

I sat thinking clearly. I had always sheltered under the mantel of my father. Now it was not enough. Something stirred, strongly resistant, an immature child-woman struggling for recognition of a dormant self? During that long time at school in England and the bleak loneliness of Yorkshire, that self had almost disappeared and become a non-person, fed on encouraging letters from home that told me what to do, with what results? Here, in my moonshine haven that other self struggles slowly towards whatever the waves, the sky could teach me. Or would there always be the child-woman crying, "Help me! Help me!"

Clouds hid the moon, and it began to drizzle. But I looked again at the darkened wave crests, leaving, still, lace patterns on the sand. Although I could not clearly see them, they were there, immutable. *Oh moon teach me to be strong, Oh sea, teach me your whispered advice.*

Now I was me, clamouring to get out, to make my own mistakes and knew I must find my own answers.

"You are a pale shadow of your father."

"I have a different shadow, which is mine."

"What of your mother?

She once went under. Am I to go under, too?

The sea and the waves and wind said: *No, Not as long as you see us, see nature in the heart of a single flower an answer to your questioning. Your answer is the quietening of a frightened mind. Remember.*

Remember what?

The girl in the silver green car drives slowly home. Forgetting already.

"I THINK BUNTING'S OVER-DOING it," my mother was saying.

"In England she was like a frightened little snail hiding in its shell," I heard my father say.

࿉

I kept asking my father to take me on one of his visits to the Veddas. The answer was always a flat "No."

"Why?"

"One has to be psychologically ready for these journeys."

"Christine's not strong enough," my mother said automatically.

"It's a different kind of strength she needs. She's still finding her feet skittering about with her friends. She needs time to lever her over the last five years away. Incredible that she had never been to a dance until she came back." He was angry with himself for letting my mother persuade him into letting me lead what he only discovered in retrospect, was an unnatural life for a young girl. I knew nothing about sex. If we saw a dog mating my mother would say, "Look the other way, Bunting." My father smoked his pipe in silence. "Never talk to strangers," she'd say repeatedly.

Sometimes a strange restlessness made me slip out of the house after dinner and drive quietly onto a deserted Galle Face Esplanade, or an empty beach to hear the sound of the sea, to see the stars, and pick out the few my father told me about: Venus, the early star; Orion's belt; red Mars, named after the god of war; the flare of the Milky Way with its misty trail of light, and wonder if, some day, they would be explored and what they would yield. When I returned home later the scent of the temple flowers planted along the drive seemed less overpowering, more pervasive, and I'd glance up at the big, friendly house above me, and think, "At last I'm home."

⁂

The telegram from Maha Oya arrived unexpectedly. Tikkiri knew where his father was. If my father came immediately, perhaps Tikkiri might be induced to lead the doctor to him. The matter was urgent.

Tikkiri's father, a Vedda murderer had escaped from the police. In the vast wastelands of the Wanni, marked on maps as Vedda territory, Tissahamy lay hidden with the cunning of a leopard.

My father turned to me and said, "How about it, Bunting? Want to come on the jungle trip of your life?" He was staring at me with a half-smile. Challenging.

"When do we go?"

"The day after to-morrow."

We hauled tents, camping-equipment, and guns, out of cupboards; old clothes and chintzy cloths for the Veddas who had no clothes. My mother and I shopped from detailed and well-used lists of food for twenty that could be carried on a fourteen-day trip.

I packed khaki trousers and shirts and the stout canvas, rubber-soled boots my father insisted on for me. My mother was troubled. She had brought me up on the principle that I was delicate and must be shielded; my father said, "Rubbish!"

⁂

The Maha Oya rest-house was an almost unknown rest house on the edge of the forest. This was the starting point of all my father's crazy wanderings.

Scraggy fowls ran in the baked compound, a man dragged a frowzy broom across the yard; the rest-house keeper ran out in a clean sarong, and a group of fifteen men who had been squatting on the cement veranda hurried to greet my father. Suddenly the tenseness was gone; he was grinning at each of them in turn, calling them by name. Twelve were his well tried carriers; but three shaggy-haired men in loin cloths broke from the group to embrace him with cries of "Our *Hudu hura* has come!" and broke into a wild frenetic dance with tangled locks swinging, bare bodies swaying, feet stamping. Only one, a strongly muscled man with hair tied back and carrying an old gun, moved away from the dancers to quietly talk with my father. Quick questions, my father's voice too low to hear, his eyes concentrated as he listened to monosyllabic answers. Then he turned to me. "I can't get a straight answer from Tikkiri, but there's no doubt that he knows where his father is."

~

Tissahamy, the Vedda outlaw, had shot his son-in-law to avenge the murder of his only daughter. He was wanted by the Police whom he had evaded for fifteen years. He was seen once by my father by firelight when the group had gathered one evening after a camp dinner in the heart of the forest.

"Who are you?"

"I am the man they call *Minee-Maruwa*, the Murderer."

"Do you know who I am?"

"You are the one they call Jungle Doctor."

~

We rose at dawn. I tied more firmly the laces of my mandatory brown canvas boots, and joined my father for the last cooked breakfast we would have for two weeks.

The night before the carriers had stacked their loads of rice, vegetables and camp equipment evenly between them, and were ready. The Veddas stood a little apart, Handuna chewing a juicy stem, Gomba pot-bellied above his loin cloth scratching a scabrous shoulder; gentle Heen Kaira looking at nothing; Tikkiri, his gun slung over one shoulder led us single file down the grey macadam road, down the slippery bank of the Maha Oya, the great river, in this, the drought season, a shimmering skin of brown water in the morning light. We had three rivers to cross to reach the hamlet of the Bintenne Veddas.

৵

Tikkiri swung ahead bare muscles rippling, my father behind him. We had not travelled more than a mile or two before sweat poured down my forehead over a face that I could not be bothered to mop. I tripped over a root; saw that my father had not slowed his pace. After that it was easier. Just one step after another, with the jungle creepers closing tighter as the path narrowed. Halfway we stopped for a swift drink of water from our flasks, then on again, until we

Gama a true Vedda

reached Gama's hut where we were to set up camp. My first camp.

The carriers worked with precision, quickly latching a tent-rope between two trees and hauling a square of canvas over it, stretched taut with tent pegs. My father sat on a deerskin, inside Gama's mud and wattle hut, while I sat on a camp chair outside.

"Look out for ticks," my father called.

We were camped by a dried-out riverbed when I saw the two lines of black ants purposefully crawling towards the tent.

"Kadias!" observed a tracker.

I leaped out of the way. My father continued to read.

"Ants," he murmured, "are a particularly interesting part of our hemisphere."

"One's just bitten me," I said sourly. With interest he watched me try to peel it off my calf. "They clutch hold with their mandibles and hang on," he said. "Keep trying; sometimes the mandible remains locked under the skin and gets infected."

"Don't scratch. About the ants… the man who wrote this book studied a long range of ants in two continuous lines scurrying in opposite directions. One line with their mouths full, the other in the opposite direction with their mouths empty. The line was 24 yards long. How long do you think this one goes?"

I scratched some more. "Thank you," I said.

"Some climbed the stalks of grain-bearing plants and shook down the seeds, others waiting below took up the fallen grains and carried them towards the granaries. But, my dear child, only to the entrance of the nest, where comrades pulled the grains inside. Now isn't that interesting?"

"Riveting."

"It's no use telling you anything! Study our ants! Learn from nature! Listen to this: 'someone tried to cheat them by scattering small china beads the size and colour of the grains. At first they were found and carried off, but the wise little creatures soon found their mistake, and left the useless beads alone.' And this, Bunting! 'The large mounds which may frequently be found at the entrances of their nests are nothing more than the rubbish heaps and kitchen middens of each establishment!"'

We had camped on the edge of the jungle not far from a large anthill when my father started on his ant book. That's how he taught me. He knew his jungles better, perhaps, than anyone in the island, but first-hand knowledge was always backed by solid facts. To experience, to enquire, to learn more, was his way of teaching me about the wildlife he loved. And what was written in his book was true I found out as I watched the two long lines of purposeful ants, jogging along in different directions, and marvelled.

We moved tent that night, my father finally conceded that to place a tent near an anthill was not the wisest of things to do. Not because of the ants, but because ants were the favourite food of the sloth bear, the most feared animal of Ceylon's jungle.

↬

Notes from my diary:

As we walked on we saw: a bunch of hair on the path - leopard excreta of a monkey. The scratching of Jungle fowl (a smooth patch); holes by roots, porcupine; holes by anthills, pangolin; for the yams of a creeper, wild boar; near anthills a bear.

Massang Alla was a lovely camp we set up by a river. Daddy-long-legs skimmed zigzagging over the water. A dragonfly paused for a second on a quivering leaf, its body gleamed as it returned to the same leaf. Yellow butterflies, and copper ones, the colour of dead leaves on the sandy banks. Small fish darting in the shallows.

A second dragonfly joins the first in coquettish fluttering though they pretend to ignore each other. Off they dart again in quick, circular flight and back, always on the same leaf; or one will fly to it, with sun-gilded wings, long, slender bodies pointing skywards, and they mate. In the evening the wind came sighing through the leaves of the trees, and passed, shredding more leaves like fallen butterflies into the stream and onto the heavy sludge thick with the litter of a hundred years.

∼

The two tents were separated from the river with its skein of water by a rocky coppice. As the moon rose a forest eagle owl cried in one of the great kumbuk trees by the river. It was hard to sleep with the thousand noises. A far-off deer cried in pain; a dry branch cracked and fell with a rustle of leaves. Then there was stillness, and in it, a different sound.

"What's that?"

"Go to sleep. It's only a pig rooting."

The camp was quiet as I peered through a slit in the tent flap. The shaggy black shape of a sloth bear was clearly outlined against the anthill, and beside it a cub that presently suckled its mother. For a long time I watched, then crept to bed to sleep sweetly. When I woke the jungle cock was calling and mist rose over the forest.

IT WAS DIFFICULT AT first. But after a while, they, the young crowd who had grown up 6,000 miles away from me, grew used to me. And there was dancing, which changed everything. Guy was good-looking, young, good at tennis and sports, and surely the best dancer, anywhere.

"I'm hopeless," I said, stumbling.

"It's just practice," he said.

And so on lazy afternoons at Wycherley the portable gramophone was cranked, and I learned to dance, breathlessly, joyously, to the latest records, the latest dances.

࿎

When we could, at weekends, four or five of us would roar out of town to some forgotten rest-house near a river or the sea to swim, to eat, to laugh, to dance to a portable gramophone and return early as my parents insisted. For me though they were innocent enough outings, and I was naïve enough to think it was always so. Teasing, they called me Touch-me-not, behind my back, but I was still a small part of the crowd, yet not wholly with it.

Gradually my father's lectures and slides of his jungle trips had made 'going jungling' important. If there were two or three days free, a car-load would leave at two in the morning from

Colombo, and as the pink dawn hit the sky a hundred miles or more from town, we'd watch for smoke rising in a distant rise of a hill, where a woman would be seated making hoppers for wayfarers. We would watch rice-flour and coconut-water batter swirled in a pan; crack an egg on each browning hopper, swallow it with hot coffee from our flasks. Then, on again to the dusty grey-green of the forests, for the sight of a leopard, the forlorn cry of a peacock.

It was not 'jungling' as my father knew it, with his carriers and tents, and the long, long treks from camp to camp, but the nearest we could get to it.

One day, Guy asked me to marry him and I told my parents excitedly, "I'm engaged!"

My father said, "Don't be absurd, Bunting, you're both too young." and continued reading his newspaper. We were far too young everyone said, and so we were. Finally we agreed to wait a year.

❧

Shortly before the wedding which had been set for the 17th November, 1933 my eternally over-anxious parents insisted on taking me on a six- week visit to London to get my trousseau. When we returned 11 days before the wedding (the invitations had been printed in London and posted in Ceylon) Fifinella who had been in Guy's care, lay abandoned, broken in the garage, her body bruised. I felt bruised, too. Then anxious. Do I really know this so-charming man I am to marry? He's still got that gorgeous smile that touches hearts. Seven hundred people have accepted that invitation.

Let the charade go on!

At the Church of St. Michael's and all Angels I hear the Wedding March, the concerted rise of the congregation. I look at my father beside me, the bony planes of his face rigid. The wedding is a large one. The nave and aisles of the church are filled with people; faces stare towards my father and me, on his arm, as the organ breaks into the wedding march.

"Bunting," says my father.

I freeze. The baskets of flowers ordered so carefully, where are they? There are no flowers at this wedding except the ordinary ones.

"Bunting?"

Four gorgeous bridesmaids in glowing turquoise and a small flower-girl follow us up the aisle.

"No flowers," I think, petrified. "No flowers at all." Baskets of them from up-country lie wilting in some back room of the church forgotten.

"Bunting," says my father again.

Clutching my bouquet of five arum lilies against my narrow silver lamé dress - *But Mummy, he likes sophisticated clothes* - I move up the aisle on my father's rigid arm followed by my four beautiful, bridesmaids. The service passes in a dream.

And afterwards: two large marquees set on the Wycherley lawns. Where is my husband? I look round wildly but cannot see him. I lay down my bouquet to greet guests. "So young," they murmur. The arums have disappeared from the chair where I had laid them. The party goes on with its seven hundred people under the marquees in the garden.

Later, I catch sight of my also-too-young tea planter husband comforting a weeping bridesmaid at the edge of the lawn. I think I grew up, then. *This marriage* must *work. It will come right in the tea-clad hills of Herondale Estate.*

Ryan was there. He looked thoughtful, a little sad as I approached him.

"So you did it," he said with that quirky smile.

"Did what?" Knowing what he meant.

"Married the first man who asked you."

"Ryan, you always manage to annoy me…"

"I'm going away for a while," he said, "to a seminary in France. Enjoy your life on the tea estate."

And so we went away like two children to the Estate. To the tea-covered hills with my twenty-four year old husband – neither of us ready for marriage. To the Planter's bungalow my father had built for us. Shut out whatever happened before, I think. I slowly began to grow up, even to become outwardly composed, but never enough to catch up with my friends anywhere.

1934-1942

The War Years

Only the dead have seen the end of war
- Plato -

I WOKE TO THE lingering call of the muster horn reverberating across the hills. My husband had already left to see the mustering of the Tamil labour force.

I could sleep some more, for surely I needed it. But the sun shone in the window, and the sky was blue with a clarity we never saw in Colombo.

❧

We called it *Herondale* and though there were no herons there, it seemed that all the birds of the Kandyan Kingdom gave it music, and the lie of the land was wild and sweet with its encircling hills and patches of forest where wild boar roamed, and it was said, a leopard.

My father had bought the estate for its beauty and the single waterfall that gurgled through the valleys and fell singing over polished rocks, while above, dragonflies hovered and clouds of yellow butterflies fluttered on their way towards Sri-Pada, the holy mountain.

Here, too young, over-protected at home, my schools, my isolated holidays and knowing nothing of real life, or how to run a house, I went to live when I married.

The estate bungalow was carved out of the hillside and the raw bank hung in its lee. The kitchen window facing the gashed hillside showed in bas-relief the undulating crest of the forests, with kites forever wheeling and crying their challenge. There was no refrigerator, no electricity. At night five polished brass lamps traced strange patterns of shadow and twilight in the main rooms. For the rest, darkness, unless a candle, a lamp, or a torch lit a dark passage. The bathroom held a tiny oil lamp, its cone, gold in a violet haze, enough to highlight a stray tree frog clamped against a wall.

There was no telephone.

It did not worry me that the land was steep, its rainfall one of the heaviest in the island. No matter how abundantly fertilizer was forked in, it leached out of the soil leaving skeleton roots searching and tea bushes hungry. Yet for the sake of the waterfall and the kites, and the ferns that sprang soft feathers from rocky outcrops, and a thousand indefinable reasons, the estate continued to exist, though when drains overflowed, and parts of the road were washed away, and sudden rock-falls made the estate rain-locked, it had a new identity.

∻

Again the muster horn wails over the tea-greened hills and valleys of *Herondale* and I wake to a new day on this gentle tea estate I have begun to love. Guy is already pulling on khaki shorts, a white shirt, ready to go down to the factory. Barefooted I run to the windows, throw them wide to let the sunshine in; outside it gilds green tea-fields flushed with new life. Here I could get life into proportion. Grow up in my own way. Guy and I were going to be all right.

I call for Anthony our only help – cook, houseman – everything at fifteen rupees a month which was considered reasonable - to boil up a drum of hot water for my bath. And so a new day begins. And I have much to learn.

∻

I learned to love the rain-soaked hills, to listen to wind whip the great shade trees of the estate, and know on quiet moonlit nights the silence of the sleeping tea. The rain had different voices; I could almost hear the fecundity of this land where the tea sprouted overnight and the bittersweet smell of growth crept into the house and into our damp books.

Even though I realize a fortune must have been spent on the visit to England, the building of *Herondale* bungalow, the buying of a boring car to replace the irreplaceable Fifinella, and finally the size of the wedding which I would infinitely have preferred to be smaller, I have a strange feeling that my father believed it was time his over-protected daughter got on with life: faced difficulties.

One day when I was alone, two strangers, one with a bicycle, arrived exhausted on the doorstep. They spoke quietly. One had slept with the wife of the other. He hid in our jungle knowing this was a route the other took at this time on his bicycle. When he rushed down the slippery track to attack, the man said, "Why do you want to kill me? Is such a woman worth it?" I drove them to the village police station where they were let off with a warning.

The weekly tennis meets at the Planters' club, was the only contact *Herondale* had with its neighbours. On a nearby estate, an English planter was shot by his head clerk, and a man came running to say the drains ran red with blood. They had placed him in a bathtub until the police arrived.

Two weeks passed, then "Tuesday," remarks my husband, "Good! It's time you were introduced to the Tennis Club. You'll like it," he adds cheerfully. It is the first time I have been there.

That evening he is soon on the courts, a far better tennis player than the rest. Wives sit in a row along the cement verandah, watching. "He's good," one wife says to me kindly. Another leans across and says icily, "Christine, we never got a thank-you for our wedding present."

"Oh! I'm sorry!" is all I can say. I had understood that he had written to thank all the people he knew and so I did not.

"Nor did we!" chime in others. I lower my head in confusion.

As dusk fell, one of the younger wives put on a dance record.

"Guy! Come Guy! Tap-dance for us." Fred Astaire was the idol of the moment. Guy was good. Very good: feet stamping out the rhythm on the ping-pong table. Leaping off to grab me and swing me round in a swirl.

Then, walking out to the car, he puts a possessive arm round my shoulders, "Great, isn't it?"

I am quiet as we drive back to the estate through a cloud-burst. "What's the matter?"

"Nothing."

It was pelting with rain now; our garage, coyly based below the rise on which the house was situated meant we would be soaked. Suddenly I began to laugh as I ran drenched, up to the house with its paraffin lamps welcoming, and soaked logs spluttering in its only fireplace, in the dining room. This was our home and its warmth closed in around me. Tomorrow I would begin to write to the people left out of our 'Thank you' list.

In 1935 a malaria epidemic hit the plantations in the central hills. In Kandy, Gampola and the neighbouring areas every hospital was overcrowded. Patients slept on the floor, passages, anywhere they could. Planters' wives joined the crusade to help at small clinics that mushroomed to dispense anti-malarial tablets and advice. In our district the clinic was at the planters' tennis club.

Six weeks after our wedding we drove down to Wycherley. I am, I discover, pregnant. I also have malaria; a dangerous combination. We drove past people lying in highways, some dying, one dead. The owner of the next estate had cerebral malaria and shot himself. I developed malignant malaria. The mosquitoes bred fast. Braziers of red hot charcoal sprinkled with pungent anti-mosquito powder were not effective. They bit, until our faces, limbs, were swollen and patterned with bumps.

At the beginning of what turned out to be one of the island's worst malarial epidemics to hit the mid-country uplands, Quinine and Chloroquin were the most common anti-malarial drugs prescribed, but I, with the sudden burning temperatures and icy chills of malignant malaria could not take them. Instead I was ordered by my father to take arsenic, ten drops of it, bitter, a little frightening, in water. And: "No driving," which would make me a virtual prisoner on an estate with no access to a telephone.

～

Back on Herondale, I was appalled to find how fast the epidemic spread. No way could I sit back and do nothing about it. And so, when possible, I would drive out to a clinic to help, and return almost unnoticed.

Pregnancy? I am not ready for it.

A what-do-I-do sort of feeling. Frankly, unready. Both of us a little shocked. There is not much conversation about it. My mother gives me, too late, a book by a famous French gynaecologist on sex and pregnancy. I do not read it. Very boring, at this stage… I walk for the first time of my life for pleasure. (Remember the walk-to-the windmill and back when I was at school in England, in lieu of sports which my parents thought I was not strong enough to do?) Now I notice small things. Down at the tadpole pool (called Taddy-pool) I watch dragonflies and butterflies above the splashing, lashing water. On a bank behind the house a vegetable garden has been planted. The loamy, sloppy red soil washes away, replaced with new soil to be washed away again. I study books on up-country gardening, with minor results. Maybe I am not a very good gardener? Gradually a garden emerged from the raw soil. Young Tamil girls with shy faces bent over moist earth planting as swiftly as their parents, and grandparents had done before them. Beds were staked out, planted, and incredibly quickly produced flowers. Inside the house I faced a different kind of housekeeping from any I had ever imagined.

I am a good knitter, though. I can read while I knit. One day I will create a pool, shaped to the design of this island; and when its finished I'll plant it with blue nelun flowers, and water lilies. One day.

The malaria comes and goes with its rigors and burning fever. *Take your arsenic and ten drops of water, my dear.*

I feel misshapen and lousy with this. But the epidemic worsens. I MUST help…

"Don't let water collect in your drains," we were told. Easier said than done in areas where the rainfall was over 200 inches of water a year; 225 at Nawalapitiya.

࿇

Occasionally we had to get away. One Sunday we drove to Horawapatana, beyond Kandy. It was peaceful there, with wide swathes of jungle, paddy land, beyond, distant hills. No rain had fallen there for some time and there was the smell of dry earth, the susurrance of cicadas rasping, the chatter of birds.

Then, a gust of wind rose, a flare of powdery dust; the harsh rattle of gunshots into a wave of snipe over the paddy fields. The smell of cordite. A triumphant "got them!" and the spell was broken.

I was in no mood for the red-hot curry lunch, restless during the sleep hour afterwards, ready to return through Kandy. But there we stopped, for *Henry V* was on at the local cinema. Then the first spasm hit and then another.

"The curry perhaps," I said, then "I've got to get out."

What was the matter? I didn't know. "Uncle Noel, please," I said. "Quickly, Sunningdale Gardens."

My father's youngest brother Noel was one of the island's most brilliant Gynaecologists and Obstetricians. I don't know what made me think immediately of him, for he was ever resentful of the older brother who paid for his studies, and we seldom met.

He and his wife, Muriel, an ex-nurse, lived quietly in a small house in Kandy. He opened the door, followed by a small black dog, took one look at me and called sharply "Muriel," I heard the word "emergency."

I do not remember much, but after what seemed a long time, my uncle gave sporadic incisive instructions while he stood up.

"Your baby is safe. You have only just been saved from a miscarriage. We're phoning your mother to come up and take you by train to Colombo."

I tried to say thank you, but he held up his hand and shook his head. I shall never be able to thank sufficiently that quiet, lonely man so different, but no less caring than his more glamorous brother. I have often thought of that day when he paid back his debt to his brother. He had not thought of that when he took me in. A lonely, childless man with a passionate love for his little black stray dog Nellie.

❧

Parents visit about once a fortnight now. We visit Colombo frequently. Guy has been invited on another snipe shoot. That evening I go into early labour pains. Anne was an eight-months' baby, born unexpectedly when I was staying with my parents at Wycherley, as I was not quite well. Guy returned from a shooting trip with friends while I was in labour. Anne weighed 5 lbs. Beautiful. With perfectly manicured fingernails. Do they still look like that?

She was a tiny baby. My mother gave me a book on mothercraft and I went back to *Herondale* with Anne and an excellent ayah, happily, knowing little about babies or motherhood.

Back at the estate of the flighting birds I drove away the big fears, and did not acknowledge the small ones. Instead I listened unafraid for individual sounds to drown an eternal loneliness that perhaps came from my school at England, or some long forgotten cause. I had returned to the estate just as the monsoon struck, strident with the battle cries of storms: forked lightning against purple skies. Thunder roaring. Silence, then, punctuated by the death-drip of rain; then frogs - a harsh cacophony of sounds, jubilant, urgent.

The progeny of a million froglets spawned at 'Taddy Pool' by the waterfall.

And with the damp dawn, red mud like polished red cement Colombo floors, leeches slithering, and pulled like elastic until the suck of their mouths slackened, leaving red blood. Then a rainbow-kissed sky, and I dearly love this baby.

On a small, Baby Corona typewriter I typed my first published short story. It appeared in the Times of Ceylon. Today I came across it in a large, battered cuttings book, *The Blue Ginger Jar*.

On *Herondale* my special friend was the old tea-maker who had once made tea in great factories. He was a gentle yet proud old man, who, indoors or out, defensively wore a hat to hide his greyness. A tea-maker, he told me in his soft, unaccented voice, should be strong to pace the footage of his factory, to climb and re-climb its formidable iron stairs. He knew so many things. "Tell me!" I would begin, and he would tell me that tea dust swept off the floor of the factory was good for Barberton daisies, or that a kangani in the 'lines' had a cow and chickens and could supply me with milk and eggs. Or he would name any bird or tree I asked about: he knew them all. Only our tea made him sorrowful: he preferred not to discuss it and I respected his silence.

When the sun shone I would walk up the red-soil road that cut into the hillside and wound through the estate past banks of ferns and wild orchids. Abruptly, where the tea ended, there was nothing but undulating grassland still lush with remembered rain and heavy with a myriad leeches. It was here I always turned back, for I was no walker.

One day when mist veiled the tea, I walked much further past the patana land and came on a sudden clearing with scattered bricks and rocks and the blackened remnants of a curiously fashioned chimney. There was no sign of a house, or other buildings.

That evening I hurried to find my friend the tea maker. He stood on a jutting rock above the valley, his weather-stained hat pushed off his forehead, his back a little stooped under a sagging wool jacket. As I approached, he quickly doffed his hat with a curious sideways bow of his head and straightened.

"What is that chimney on the patanas?" I asked.

His strange, grape-green eyes brightened. "Ah, the coffee…" he said.

"Tell me - please."

"There was coffee growing here, then."

"When?"

"When I was seven or eight, perhaps."

Sixty years ago! I sat on a rock and listened. And much of it I researched later.

All the hills of Ceylon, he told me in his fractured English, were once covered with vast forests teeming with many thousands of elephants. In the reign of the great kings, maybe a thousand years ago, he said, they were corralled in stockades and trained to help build dagobas, irrigation schemes, and other great works. When the British came, elephants once again were used for construction work and in making roads, for there were no roads.

By then the vast potential of the high range forests and its rich soil had become a matter of prime importance.

About 1825 the Peradeniya Botanical Gardens near Kandy reported that coffee would do well on the hills. Land, rich, fertile land, seedlings and Government backing was available. Thousands of strong, young men rushed from Britain to clear the forests and plant their seedlings. It needed youth and strength, and a dedication such as had never been seen in the island.

The tea maker said softly, "Coffee covered our hills, and in the season, jasmine-scented white flowers covered the land like snow, and the perfume was everywhere. No one would walk under the flowers for fear of spoiling the cherries - hard green clusters of them ripening to yellow, then shining red." The tea-maker looked at our misty land, then stooping, fiercely plucked a leaf from a straggling bush at his side "Look at this, Miss! coffee grew here, too! On this estate! As well as the deserted one you saw!" He turned the leaf over and tapped it. "Look! Miss!" On the sage-green of its under-surface I saw strange copper-coloured spots.

"*Hemiliea Vastatrix*," he said quietly. "The coffee-leaf disease that killed our coffee."

It spread, first on one estate, then another, and crops dwindled until each plantation in turn was abandoned. The chimney I had seen was all that was left of an estate that had been. Yes, he had seen it as a working plantation. Long ago.

He stopped abruptly.

"Who lived here?"

My friend suddenly looked tired, and the parchment of his skin was taut. "Now it is time for Miss to go back to the house before it is dark," he said.

"Who were the people that lived there, Johnnie? Did you know them?"

"People? There was one. Alone . . . He committed suicide." Another abrupt pause. "I was only a child, then, Madam," he said with dignity. "How would I know?"

I thanked him and turning began to walk up the road. I looked back and saw him standing proud on his rock. Still gazing at the lost land. Then I remembered. His second name was a British one.

The coffee blight, *Hemiliea Vastatrix*, spread to every plantation in the island. The coffee berries dwindled, bushes wilted, ruined planters left the island, many to found coffee plantations in the new colony of British East Africa. Those who remained tried cardamoms, and cinchona used in the making of quinine, and flooded the market. Those who stayed still believed in the country, and planted tea.

~

For four, or was it five years life continued on *Herondale*, except that now here was Anne, most precious. My parents visited more often, and sometimes insisted on taking her back to Colombo with them, which made me unhappy. There was another reason.

My husband, restless with not enough work on this small estate to keep him constantly there, was away a lot. *Herondale* was not doing well. The large new factory the Visiting Agent had advised my father to build was too much of a drain on its mediocre output.

Seven years passed. Anne, needing education, stayed at Wycherley and went to Ladies' College, Colombo. And now there was war on the edge of the horizon.

Herondale could not afford to run as before. We had two choices: to sell the estate, or run it on what was called a Care and Maintenance basis, ie. the Superintendent visiting it, say, every ten days to spend two or three days checking the minimum work allotted on his previous visit. Soon World War Two began, the estate went on a Care and Maintenance scheme. There would be not enough work for a resident planter. It could be visited twice or three times a month.

At a near-breaking point in our marriage, came a visit from our hatchet-faced Visiting Agent. We invited him to lunch.

"Do you ride?" he asked turning to me abruptly.

"Yes," I said. I had learned to in England.

He already knew from my jungle articles that I was a keen jungle lover. "How would you like to live at Nagrak Estate on the Horton Plains?" There was a small British owned estate which Guy could run, and visit *Herondale* from there.

I was delighted. My father had told me about the Horton Plains, the most remote place for wildlife in the island. Anne, now eight, would go to an up-country school where she would be safe, for the island sat at the edge of an approaching war zone. Colombo was in turmoil with British troops beginning to pour in.

"Then you'll like Nagrak. It will take a few months for the changeover. Why not take a break?" he suggested.

≈

It was my father's idea to spend that break abroad.

From my father's Diary, a laconic entry: *The four of us spent five months motoring Central Europe and covered five thousand miles. It is not the same Europe we knew. We were in Austria after the German invasion, and it was not difficult to see that Vienna was not the Vienna of old. In Austria every room carried a framed photograph of Hitler. In restaurants all tables bore the Nazi flag.*

I had been given the name of a renowned dressmaker in Vienna. "Ask for her by name," I was told. When I did so, there was a sudden silence in the *salon*. "Please, Madame, do not mention her name."

"Is she not here?"

"No, Madame. Please go now." Most of the Jewish dressmakers, among thousands of others, had already been sent to concentration camps.

At Nuremberg, in a small restaurant, five helmeted men in brown uniforms and high boots thumped in with outstretched left arms: "Heil Hitler!" "Heil Hitler!" came the reply. They sat down noisily in the sudden silence of the room, and a waitress assiduously took their order. My father was becoming impatient. "Why the hell doesn't she bring our order?" "Dick, please!" whispered my mother. There was silence in the room as we walked out.

We drove over the Austrian Alps, and stayed our last night at a restaurant, which had once been a prince's shooting-box. Deep woods surrounded it, high hills rose from a bubbling stream in the valley. On the opposite bank, lay the Italian frontier. On September 3rd we went uneasily through the frontier and so, finally, to board our ship at Trieste for Colombo.

My father wrote in his diary: *"March 15th, 1939. Hitler takes Czechoslovakia."*

Earlier we had driven to Hungary, for my father yearned to see the gypsies on the plains of Hortobagy where, he had read, they originated. Far out, over lonely land where for mile after mile there was nothing but the green plains stretching towards a blue-hazed horizon, a boy in knee-breeches and a velvet waistcoat stood calling curly-haired pig with a silver horn. But my father's objective was beyond (it was always beyond). Then, suddenly he shouted, "Stop! Gypsies!" And in the distance we saw isolated in the centre of the vast plain of Hortobagy, a gypsy encampment with horses, mules grazing; caravans with smoke swirling; swarthy men in black waistcoats, bare arms; women in bright skirts. Now he was gazing out of his window enchanted, then he was springing out of the car almost before it slowed down, his camera ready when we saw the whole clan advance menacingly towards us with upraised fists and loud voices.

"Get back! Lock the door!" The driver yelled, and he backed in reluctantly. Every window now was blurred with angry faces pressed close.

"Must give them something." Opening the window a trifle he held out a note. The next moment his hand was seized and they were getting at his gold signet ring and wristwatch when the driver pulled away.

"Daddy you are crazy," I said. "We all could have been killed."

"I think I managed to get one photograph," he said.

THAT MORNING I HAD ridden fast, my hair blowing, my breath hazing in the sweet, sharp air of the vast, strict nature reserve of the high Horton Plains, the most remote, the least known area in Ceylon. We, Lightning the ex-racehorse and I, had stopped as always by Baker's Falls, its water so lucid that I could see trout moving below the surface. Ramasamy the horse-keeper, using various short cuts, levelled up, and eyed the surface thoughtfully. It was here with a bent pin and a bamboo fishing rod that he secretly, illegally, fished for trout knowing that since the war no sportsmen came.

Eight months earlier Guy and I first rode eight miles through emptiness to the lonely house on the patanas. I had been warned, "You'll be totally isolated." The only way to reach it was on horseback. Nagrak was the most remote tea estate on the island. "It's a challenge," I had said. I thought of my failing marriage and wondered whether this could be the answer – to get away, to think. But the Visiting Agent, looking at me curiously as if he understood my thoughts, broke my frowning silence.

"Good luck to you."

The car was abandoned at North Cove Estate followed by the long ride over the Horton Plains, 7,200 ft. above sea level.

The mist deepened as the plains ascended. In a far valley I saw sambhur stags and does feed, then mist-screened, vanish. I felt an enormous thankfulness to be here, where I could see them again - far from anything that could hurt me. With the war closing in on the East, the Horton Plains strict natural reserve had been closed. But Nagrak skirted its edge.

An hour later, I stopped, breathless. Through a break in an aisle of shrubs, the land dropped sheer to the low country, and far beyond, towards the southernmost tip of Ceylon, the scimitar-gleam of the sea.

The gate hung loose on its hinges. Two angry geese hissed a challenge. The small, stone-fronted house stood bravely on a ledge of wind-swept garden. There was no electricity here, no telephones, and no communication with the outside world. Two Tamil 'boys' ran the house; Perumal, the cook of half a dozen lonely British planters who had come and gone; Krishnan, lighter-skinned, with the impassive face of a Hindu godling.

Once a week two men from the estate ran down short cuts for provisions, newspapers, letters. What did one do in an emergency, I wondered briefly, as I dismounted and entered the house. There were no neighbours to call. It was here that Guy and I had to either make our marriage work- or fail.

The two young Tamil 'boys' looked after us well. Surprisingly, Perumal's cooking was superb, and nearly everything he made came from the estate. Krishnan kept the house spotless, and filled it with flowers. They were the best 'boys' I had ever had, polite, thoughtful. My husband's visits off the estate lengthened but I did not mind. I was, for the first time in a long while, at peace. There seemed rightness that I should be nestled by the high hills at a time of crisis in my time, think with a clarity I had never found before. I took strength from the surrounding hills, a simplicity in this gentle place slowly returning to what it had been, a primordial sanctuary I was privileged to see, and which never afterwards would be the same again.

One day people came from the tea factory carrying an apparently lifeless child between them, and stood silent before me. The boy, jumping over the revolving shaft of the factory turbine had caught his sarong and his leg with it. I had him carried to a spare room bed, his people silent. Splinters of bone jagged through pulp. What could I do? My mind was blank; no medical instinct guided me. Then it came back: treat for shock. Keep the patient warm. I fed him a little hot coffee laced with brandy and aspirin dissolved in it; laid sterile gauze and cotton wool on the wounds, had a blanket to cover him, two towel-wrapped empty whisky bottles of hot water alongside him. Quietly, his people used to emergencies, made a stretcher of sacks with poles to carry him over the patanas to the nearest road where transport would take him to hospital. Miraculously, he survived.

But there were bad times too... when fear replaced exaltation...

Twice a month I would be alone for three or four days. When the wind grew hostile, people changed, and I'd sit at my small typewriter and write with the wet wood flaring and hissing in the red brick fireplace behind me, the wind shrieking, and the ghost trees outside bending until they could break.

One night I had a fever and went dinnerless to bed. The boys were restless that night, and I wondered if the wind-season affected the labour force also. A fire crackled in the bedroom, and for a while I watched flames splutter and spark up the chimney. Then putting down my book fell into a half-sleep from which I woke abruptly...

Firelight shone on the slowly turning doorknob, and as the door opened, I saw Krishnan as if he were sleep-walking come slowly towards my bed, and stand staring, a lighted candlestick in his hand.

I lay still, my heart beating, my voice quiet I asked, looking straight into his eyes. "What's the matter, Krishnan?"

For a moment, silence, then the burning stare of his eyes quietened. "I came to see if Madam is alright," he said.

"Thank you, I am well," I said quietly "Now go back to your quarters." There was a moment's stillness, then he turned and left.

It might never have happened. In the time of the wind people became a little mad, they said.

৵

When I was there, the *nilloo*, said to bloom every seven years, bore flowers white, pink, lavender and purple along a six-mile bridle track. They flowered from a few feet off the ground while some blossoms reached above the heads of the horses. The heady scent of them brought bees buzzing, and as the berries ripened, jungle fowl from far places came to eat the berries and staggered drunk just off the bridle track.

Long ago herds of elephants roamed the high hills. No longer. But in the stables I found an old wicker carrying-chair with a wicker hood and four long poles attached for carrying. The only other woman said to have lived on Nagrak was the old mother of a planter, who used it often. One day she was being carried along the *nilloo* trail when a large elephant confronted them. The carriers dropped their load and were about to run when she shouted to them, "Lift! GO ON!" and the elephant disappeared.

৵

Once after a rare visit to my parents in Colombo, I returned by train to the Pattipola station, sixteen miles from Nagrak. Ramasamy with Lightning met me on a late afternoon of driving mist. A little distance away I saw a stocky woman in a safari suit and a revolver in a holster at her belt, mount, shout orders to her syce.

As I mounted Lightning she called, "From Nagrak, aren't you? Dr. Spittel's daughter? Read his books. Jolly good, I thought.

It's a rotten night to be going up in this fog to Nagrak. Stop the night at The Farm and travel on in the morning. Name's Palliser."

I thanked her gratefully for it would not be good riding back to Nagrak as night approached. Mounting Lightning I followed her through the mist half a mile or so to a rondavel of circular huts with conical thatched roofs.

"Read your jungle articles," she said, "Like them. So… Dr. Spittel's daughter, eh? How d'you like Nagrak?"

"Love it."

"Where's your husband?"

"On a part-time job at Nawalapitiya, he's back tomorrow." She walked me to the door of one of the smaller rondavels, some distance from what was obviously theirs, and unlocked a heavy wooden door. "I'll send over a jug of hot water, a hot water bottle for tonight. Come on up when you're ready for a drink and supper." She marched off and I heard her shouting orders as she disappeared into the mist.

The inside of the circular hut, musty as if it had not been used for a long time was cold, colder than any place I could remember. Heavy wooden shutters enclosed it. In the light of a big torch Mrs Palliser had left, I lit a kerosene lamp. Its pallid light glimmered over a rough, heavily blanketed bed, a side table with a basin and ewer. Shivering with cold, I pulled on an extra sweater, a jacket, and finally made my way by torchlight to the Palliser main lodge. On the back of a chintz-covered settee I saw a magnificent leopard skin.

"The leopard with the record seven inch pad?" I asked her. It was.

She gave me sherry; she and her husband steadily drank rum throughout the evening. Hadn't they once been rumrunners on the Jamaican route?

Captain Pallisser was the milder of the two. For all his truculence and bleary blue eyes that might once have been fierce. Mrs. Pallisser had changed into an African Kanga, but it made her bark of a voice no softer. Yet the conversation was good –

fascinating. I listened mute as they told their tales of the sea and far islands, and there formed before my eyes a picture of a time when they were young and daring, and nothing mattered except the feel of the wind in the sails and the scent of danger.

Time was unimportant. It was near midnight when we sat down to a candlelit dinner, a surprisingly splendid one, with crystal, polished silver, and a superb meal of trout followed by roast lamb, home grown vegetables and a cheese savoury.

I said goodnight, walked back through the icy path to my hut, and fell at last into an exhausted sleep, abruptly wakened by the sound of a large animal sniffing round the hut. No way was I going to open the heavily shuttered windows or peer through the door. When I rose the following morning, there were clear footprints round the hut, but the hut had been circled so many times I could not be sure what they where. A dog's footprints? But no dog could be so large. A leopard? I would have been rather pleased at that, though I knew it could not be. Then I saw Mrs. Pallisser walk towards me with a pack of dogs scattering about her. Leading them was the largest dog I had ever seen. I still cannot remember what breed it was. It had come from very far away.

❧

1942 came quietly. My parents' letters grew shorter. Up here I felt a curious detachment about the reality of the war. While people were dying, what was I doing up here?
A brief letter came from my father.

Time only for a short letter. Mummy has been asked to head the Red Cross Society here. This is her field, and I know she'll do it superbly. The British community has been advised to send their wives and children to South Africa as soon as possible. Tension increases, but I doubt if Ceylon will really be in trouble.

I walked that day in a forest near the house. Above me, high in the branches, the black shapes of furry bear monkeys kept pace, relentlessly grunting. The leader of the pack slid down a tree trunk and walked parallel with me so close that I could see its fangs.

For a moment we stood almost face-to-face, perhaps twelve feet apart, with the thick brush not quite separating us. Then with a final grunt he melted into the undergrowth.

It was almost dusk when I returned and turned on the old battery radio. A harsh voice grunted, "Trincomalee in the island of Ceylon was bombed last night by the Japanese."

≈

Roads web the plains now, then there were only footpaths and bridle tracks, and no time or possibility to get in touch with anyone. I only knew I must leave immediately for Colombo and my parents. There would be things to do there. And one thing was clear. My marriage was over.

Already life on the sweet, wild plains with the mist rising, and the land stretching blue to the frail lights of the Dondra Lighthouse at the southern-most part of the island, was behind me as I hurriedly packed and gave instructions for the rest to be forwarded.

Some instinct told me it was forever.

I woke on that last night at two in the morning almost suffocated by smoke. Along the skirting board of the wall adjoining the fireplace a thin red line of fire crawled devouring the wall. Miraculously, people appeared and with axes, tore at the kabook walls till the entire house seemed filled with rubble and dust, and the acrid smell of burning.

A log from the front room fireplace had fallen onto the skirting board of the wall that connected with the bedroom. When I left the despoiled home that had sheltered and strengthened me, I knew that a part of my life was over.

COLOMBO HAD CHANGED ALMOST overnight. Loops of twisted barbed wire and men in khaki blocked roads. The racecourse where we had watched so many races, was a heavily camouflaged aerodrome, and Wycherley, with a white cross painted on the red tiled roof of the nursing home, was now in a strict Security Zone. Our gates by order are padlocked and chained nightly at seven! Many buildings were requisitioned and camouflaged. Our road is cordoned off with sentries at either end. Troops everywhere. Army vehicles thundering along the town streets; the Museum where I had done so much research, strange in its camouflage coat. The city filled with officers, troops, and yet more arriving daily; people hurrying in their thousands to the hills in over-loaded cars, buses, coaches, bullock carts, bicycles, and on foot, out of Colombo.

I ran into the study where my parents sat, tensely. They had not known how to get in touch with me, had tried phoning the estate on the edge of the Hortons where the car had been parked, and heard that the planters who had been there had gone.

We talked for a long time that evening, of life and death and courage and fear, and I was closer that night to my parents than ever before.

Gradually the tone of our talking had changed. For the first time they spoke to me as an adult. Had the Hortons changed me that much? My mother seemed to accept it more readily than my father, who sat frowning from time to time as if he could not wholly understand the change, nor like it.

"It's been difficult imagining you managing alone up there, with the winds and the moods of the place."

"You taught me that nature could be the best company," I said.

"Weren't you afraid? It would be unnatural if you weren't."

"Who taught me not to run when that elephant charged us at Bintenne?"

"That's not an answer!" he said impatiently. "That's a typical woman answer, a non sequitur. Why," he said, "are we talking of small, forgotten fears, when the world is in chaos?"

There was no answer.

I looked at my mother and smiled, two women in understanding.

"You must be tired, darling," she said, rising. "Come, shall we all go to bed?"

Next day, on the morning of the 5th of April, the Japanese bombed Colombo.

೨

My parents were already in the nursing home where patients had been transferred to mattresses on the concrete-roofed, ground floor corridors. My father was quietly reassuring. I saw my mother stooping to speak to each patient, answering worried questions, giving a quiet order to a nurse now and then. For the first time I saw her strong, transformed into the doctor she was. Around us anti-aircraft guns boomed, and Japanese planes flew close above the nursing home.

The patients were quiet, except for a low whimper, a whisper now and then.

"I'm going up to the balcony to see what's happening," my father said at last. Running to the top of the stairs I saw him standing on the balcony, his face turned in anger at the black planes, whose bombs crashed on what used to be the racecourse.

Then it was over – for how long?

~

In the early war years one morning a man in his forties with a child's gamine face and thinning curls stood shyly on the front veranda of Wycherley with a large brown paper parcel under his arm.

He was David Paynter, the son of missionaries, a gentle recluse and artist who had been hung eleven times on the prestigious 'line' of the Royal Academy of Art.

He asked, diffidently, if he could paint my father's portrait; to attempt to capture, he said shyly, 'the soul' of a man he deeply revered.

What was he to wear?

"Whatever you're happiest in, Sir."

My father came downstairs dressed in his rough jungle clothes. The faded khaki jacket and trousers, the ancient hat and to complete it the felt-covered water bottle slung over his shoulder, that David had specifically asked for.

On the front veranda of Wycherley the portrait was painted against a soft background jungle both men knew from memory. Richard was a good sitter, he relaxed, and his thoughts, concentrated on his forests, grew soft with memory as David painted with absorbed, sure strokes. The portrait was finished in three days.

~

Ceylon was vulnerable. The Japanese attacks brought massive troops surging in. I knew then I could not remain uninvolved. My mother, head of the Red Cross Unit in Colombo was deeply involved; my father, honorary surgeon for the Marines could in addition to his ordinary work be called at a moment's notice to any part of the island for an emergency. Every day the newspapers appealed for temporary women assistants. At one unit at what was the Colombo Museum I applied for an interview – without telling my parents - and was told to present myself.

I walked into the office of the interviewing officer of Command Headquarters with my baby "Smith Corona" typewriter and stood in front of his desk unconfidently.

Quick eyes flicked over me. "What's that you've got there?"

"My typewriter."

I heard a muffled titter of laughter behind me.

"You can put that away. Any previous jobs?" No.

"Shorthand?" No. "What's your speed?" he asked. I had no idea. I just typed rather fast with two fingers.

Led to a 27" typewriter I sat my five-minute test and left, my cheeks burning.

When the letter came, I had to tell my parents I had been engaged as a Class III T.W.A. at Army Command Headquarters, starting from the next day.

"You WHAT?"

I handed the letter to my father.

He studied it, frowning, then chuckled. "Good God! They must be mad! But I'm proud of you, Bunting. I think, though, that you should show them you can do better than that Grade Three."

My mother looked worried, "All those men around…" she said, vaguely.

All over the island girls, some as inefficient as I was, rushed to join up as TWA's, or in whatever capacity they were needed. Relatively few of us were trained. Gradually those who were dedicated learned.

The Camp Commandant, Major Main, for whom I worked was a kindly, thickset Scot with humorous blackcurrant eyes set in apple-red cheeks. His job was to register and take particulars of every officer who arrived in the island. It would be my job to do much the same in a limited way.

There was little time to talk with my parents. I rose early, had breakfast, and went to work with passionate dedication. I practised touch typing in every spare moment I had. I was quietly improving, managing every now and then to slip in a new word or phrase or two of shorthand when he was dictating a letter. At home in bed I went over the typewriter keys in my mind. When I fell asleep, exhausted, I dreamed of typewriter keys; started the morning always with a Gregg shorthand book taken surreptitiously to office. Major Main never said a word. The lassie was trying to improve. But one day he broke out techily: "Och, and you're a bonny lassie, but you'll never make a guid secretary."

Later I rose to be a Brigadier's secretary in another branch. Top-Secret discussions took place there. A Lieutenant Colonel stormed into the office of the Brigadier one day and said, "The xxxxxx has been sunk. I stood on the headland at Trinco (Trincomalee) and watched it go down." The whole aspect of the war turned then; and the tide of it could turn anywhere.

In the quiet office under the Bo tree, files became more Top Secret, and hours of work, irrelevant. Often I would sit in my office until it grew dark to finish something.

Do your part In-the War Effort! roared the posters of Sir John Tarbat. *Go to the dances for the troops!*

Seven year old Ann had been sent for safety to a school in the hills. I missed her badly, I had told my parents the story of my marriage and divorce, and had their backing. I had no feelings about the past. No feelings about anything. But I hurt.

I hurt, and wanted to drift, wanted to be a sort of Mata Hari, anything... it didn't really matter. I was even interviewed discreetly at a hotel, and we hadn't gone far when I realised 'they' had instantly assessed that I was obviously unsuitable. Not the sort of girl who could stand having my fingernails pulled out, and would probably reveal all at the first twinge of pain.

On the 9th April there was the second air raid on Colombo The screech of sirens seemed to come from the sky over our roof. Panicking I started to run. Where were my parents? They would go straight to the nursing home to help move the patients in the upstairs rooms to the safe area on the ground floor. Nurses and attendants were busy carrying patients on stretchers. Downstairs in a corridor with a concrete roof, my parents I found were helping settle patients on mattresses, reassuring them, making them as comfortable as they could. My mother moved among them quietly organizing, speaking to a patient here, another there, comforting, touching a hand, whispering a word of reassurance with the rest. She knew the case history of every one though she did not practice.

As for myself, I couldn't have cared less what happened to me, as an individual. I went to the dances for other troops - nice young men, most of whom danced well. And while they danced - superbly, some of them - they held dreams in their eyes of other girls at home, wives, girl-friends. And when the voiceless dance ended, they drifted away to their friends on the waiting lines, with a civil nod of the head for a quick thank you. They were little more than school kids, some of them. And I was glad to have spent an emotionless evening with them, for I was emotionless myself.

There were the Officers' Mess dances. Different. More demanding. Sometimes difficult. I was on tricky ground here, for they were more sophisticated and I less capable of dealing with some of them.

Once my mother invited two young Dutch officers she had met to lunch with us at Wycherley. They were nice, came from good homes, politely asked me out. After the second outing they spoke shyly yet formally, "We are very sorry, we shall not be going out with you again-" "No! Please, it has nothing to do with you. You are a very nice girl. Too nice. Frankly, we are men; we need women. You are not the type, and so..."

❧

At home at Wycherley, the atmosphere had become chilly. The Officers' Mess dances and dances for the troops, and notices to *Do Our Bit* and go to these harmless enough dances made my parents horrified. Their only daughter, their only child, was going out to dance with people they did not know; returning to climb over the gate at midnight because they were locked at seven, being in a restricted area.

"For God's sake, Bunting, are you mad? What's come over you?"

For God's sake, my beloved parents, let me be! For the first time in my life I feel liberated. And if you can't trust me, it's too bad, because there's nothing for you to feel bad about, and nothing I feel bad about so let it be!

My parents were worried sick. Night after night I would go out, returning when our road was closed, our gates locked by order, and having to climb the locked gates. My parents received anonymous letters. "Why do you let your daughter go out?" they said in harsher language. My father showed them to me, his face pale with anger.

"I don't go over the edge," I said, bursting with rage. "If you can't trust me, that's too bad," and I flounced out of the library.

So much happened then to girls I knew. Some simply disappeared – to marry or become engaged and then to be left; to go on dancing until their feet hurt, and their hearts hurt, maybe until another man came along; a few to disappear.

It was a heady time, nevertheless, and I guessed its dangers; a time for caution, when nothing except war seemed important. What my parents did not know was that there was nothing for them to be afraid of. Under the bravado there was still an area which remained aloof. I had been hurt badly. And Anne whom I missed, my beloved daughter, was still in the hills at school.

◈

I met Alistair in the twilight of a curfew-darkened veranda after an Officers' Mess dance where four or five of us, friends, lingered talking.

At the end of the passage a tall, slim figure with an early-balding head and an immaculately polished Sam Brown belt across one shoulder emerged and stood alone.

"Alistair Wilson, just come out of Burma," someone said. "Alistair, come over and join us."

The thin, youthful-looking captain with the neat moustache and steady, grey eyes that met mine directly had something that made me look at him again as he firmly took my hand.

He said, "What can I get you to drink?"

"Ginger beer," I said. "Please."

A flicker of surprise. An unusual drink in those days when others were holding warm, once-iced whiskys, gins or whatever.

Major Alistair MacNeil Wilson

"How was Burma?" they asked eagerly.

There was nothing more than that, the first day. He spoke briefly about his time in Burma, lightly fending off questions with a softness in his voice that held the rolling r's of Scotland. It was the voice that held me, not the too-casual words to which I hardly listened, but knew instinctively hid some greater story.

We did not meet again for three months. But I remembered his voice.

The second time I met Alistair was at the Mount Lavinia Hotel where I had driven alone to look at the sea to watch the sun go down. I wanted quietness.

He was there, alone too, for the same reason. We laugh as we discover this. It is a clear, warm night, and we sit on the terrace feeling we have known each other for a long time.

Alistair and I were quietly married at St. Andrews Scots Kirk on December 11, 1944. My parents were there and Vera del Tufo, the Matron of Honour for me, an Army officer friend of Alistairs. Afterwards, a small reception at Wycherley for a few special friends. Then we drove away to the hills where another friend had offered her beautiful Nuwara Eliya home for our honeymoon.

My parents were delighted. They loved Alistair deeply. There was something special about him.

Anne now brought back to Ladies' College Colombo from the up- country school she disliked, was also delighted, and loved him dearly.

My husband, Alistair Wilson.

THE WAR WAS OVER. The war in Europe in May, 1945, the war with Japan in August of that year.

Alistair's last army posting was as Officer Commanding Troops, Diyatalawa and Nuwara Eliya. Set in the high hills of Uva, 4,000-5,000 feet above sea level, there was apart from the Army and Navy camps which came within the O.C. Troops' administration, another for the rehabilitation of men released from Japanese prisons. Here, in quiet, beautiful surroundings, rest and recreation were offered, medical attention, and understanding. A secret unit by itself, it was a sensitive area few people knew anything about outside the camp.

Their privacy was absolute. Occasionally, while walking through the village below our house, I would see a few of its men slouch spiritlessly past the clustered boutiques. What should I do? Smile a quiet Good Morning? No, do nothing, I was told. It was a strange feeling. I seldom saw any of them even at the small cinema or church.

We, in an old, renovated house set high above the road and reached by raw steps carved out of the hillside were always aware of it.

As we sat together on the veranda of that first day, I watched my husband, his face young, thoughtful in the smoke of his pipe. The clean scent of Eucalyptus trees drifted across the valley, and the first lights of the camp we could not see would begin to glitter.

"I was one of the lucky ones that got away," he said at last.

"Tell me, if you feel like it -" I said. "The Burma part."

He said "The part I don't talk about…"

He had a beautiful speaking voice. Now he spoke in harsh, short sentences.

"I was one of about twenty young officers selected for a crash course in Burmese and jungle warfare. We were sailing on a troopship on a Top Secret mission towards Burma when Rangoon fell: the Burmese Prime Minister had joined forces with the Japanese. We were diverted to India; our original group of young officers scattered." Alistair, his feet swollen with foot rot was immediately hospitalized and an overworked Army doctor scribbled on his bed head ticket, *Unfit for duty in the tropics. Recommended for immediate repatriation.* "Instead, through some mix-up," Alistair said, "I found myself sailing on a ship to Rangoon, isolated from any unit. My cabin number was thirteen."

Rangoon was a deserted city when he reached it. Houses burned, shops were looted, its people gone. A dog howled in the shadow of a still-smoking house. A child lay dead in a side road. Everywhere there was the stink of cordite and corruption. Cut off from his original group, he belonged to no one. Only a scattering of mixed army personnel remained. A Brigadier detailed him and a team of five officers and senior NCO's to immobilize as far as possible the harbour area and oil facilities as best they could and report to Head Quarters further north. Accompanied by a sergeant, he was one of the last to leave Rangoon.

There was a long pause. I watched him as he leant back in his chair, his eyes thoughtful. "I have no idea what his name was!" he says incredulously. "No recollection whatever!"

They, the unnamed sergeant and he, rode in a requisitioned jeep out of the deserted town past a ragged line of escaping men, women and children, carrying what possessions they could, too tired, too bewildered to cry.

Bodies lay along the side of the road. A sporadic burst of fire blew off the top of a man's head. Japanese planes zoomed overhead, firing. The jeep sputtered and cut out.

The two men began to walk, pushing now into heavy jungle through which the sunlight never came, only a deep, green twilight, with lianas twisting, and unseen creatures rustling out of sight; then the bamboo forest, he said, "and the growl of a tiger. Then a voice shouting in Japanese."

They had stumbled into a small Japanese lookout post and were bundled into a makeshift hut of rough timber and thatch ineptly secured. Next morning at dawn they would be transferred to a big P.O.W. camp from which escape would be practically impossible.

As the small camp grew quiet the two men watched through a gap in their shelter. They had eased a stave from their hut, and another had been loosened. In the moonlight they saw their guard remove his helmet, scratch his head, and presently fall asleep, the helmet at his side. A smart hard blow on the head with the stave put him into a very deep sleep from which he probably never awoke. The two slipped into the night and freedom.

I guess what happened. I have no knowledge of this other Alistair of whom he speaks.

I ask my husband, "What were they like, your captors?"

"They bandaged a wound on my leg, and gave us food," he said. "They were young," he added.

The stars shine bright in the Diyatalawa sky. Venus, the first star of the evening, nestles above the sickle of an early moon; Jupiter, and Mars, the red one; the spangled veil of the Milky Way. Somewhere a nightjar calls, and another answers.

෴

In Glasgow a mother gets a telegram from her son, dated March 1942, from Myitkyina, Burma. Shortly afterwards the B.B.C.

reports heavy fighting in the area with Myitkyina totally wiped out by the Japanese. There is no further news of her son for six months.

From Alistair's Diary:

> *I have thought much about those six months of jungle warfare, now with one unit, then another, carrying out orders. Sick with malaria, dysentery; listening to the drone of planes, the intermittent spatter of guns. Noise, and sudden uneasy silences. My mother's blue leather-covered Bible goes with me everywhere, though I seldom read it.*

Alistair will not speak, even to me, of these things. It was another kind of war. Too much torture seen, too much death. Thousands of others who had gone the same journey had not survived.

Six months later, reporting at last to his unit in Calcutta, riddled with malaria and dysentery, he saluted his receiving adjutant, and collapsed.

"I was one of the lucky ones that got away," Alistair said.

From our house now, I caught a glimmer of light from the Camp where British ex-prisoners of war tried to forget their memories.

~

We were happy, and young enough to use every moment of our free time to drive out to the Ella waterfalls, or to the low-country jungles. But the war was over, the troops, leaving, and Alistair, discharged from his duties, would be leaving with Anne and me for Glasgow.

Before we left there was one thing my father had to do for us.

He took us both to visit his Veddas. In camp I watched the two men smoke pipes together in absolute harmony. Alistair adapted easily to this environment, helped my father set up tents without seeming to do so. They were like two boys together, swapping stories, laughing, then serious when they spoke of war. This was scrub jungle; vastly different from the primeval jungle Alistair had known. What was that bird? What are these tracks in the sand? What are the names of the Veddas sitting around us? Which one is Tissahamy's son?

The Veddas clustered round him eagerly, for they had never seen a *Hudu Hura* who was indeed paler than the *Hudu Hura* himself.

Then it was time to go. Alistair went ahead to Colombo in his staff car. Anne, nearly eleven, and I with a mass of luggage were to follow in a naval ambulance with two nursing sisters.

A thin drizzle glossed the road that afternoon and the hills were misted as we approached the Ginigatenne Pass with its frightening drops.

Round a slippery corner the ambulance driver braked. The car slowly skidded left, then right, then left and off the road. Noise; someone shrieking. The thought "I'm sorry I couldn't say goodbye," as the vehicle went over.

I lay doubled against the door with the broken seat partly over me. A bloodied hand reached out and a British voice, said, "Easy now, just grip my hand - That's it!"

Five of us stood on a steep slope among the tea bushes. Beside us, 100 feet off the road, the Ambulance held by a small sturdy Dadap tree lay on its hood, its wheels still spinning. Below us a drop of three hundred feet glimmered in mist. Anne stood, hunched and shivering beside me. One of the British nurses held a handkerchief to her mouth; she had lost two front teeth; the other nurse stood silent, in shock. The sick bay attendant had a cut on his arm; the driver sulked. I seemed to be all right, except for a cut caused by a sharply pruned tea bush. My back ached, but I shrugged it off, not knowing that it was to monitor my life.

1946-1948

A Writer Awakes

A word is dead
When it is said,
Some say.
I say it just
Begins to live
That day.
- Emily Dickinson -

ONE GREY OCTOBER DAY in 1946 Alistair, Anne and I arrived by train from London to Glasgow, my husband's city.

His mother's letter to us in Ceylon when we were married had begun: "Naturally, your letter about your marriage came as a shock to us. But what's done is done…We look forward to your return."

I suggested we should stay in a small private hotel until we were settled, but Jim, Alistair's beloved eldest brother wrote, "Our mother would be most upset if you did not stay at Burnbank Terrace." I was worried not for myself, but for them. There were bound to be problems. I remembered my parents' unhelpful philosophical advice. "Take everything as it comes," suggested my father. "You must wrap up well and keep warm," urged my mother.

Fog swirled over the city as we were driven past ghost ruins of bombed buildings and blackened churches, ruins such as I had never imagined. I closed my eyes for a moment, and Alistair quietly put his hand over mine. What was there to say? Glasgow had gone through some of the heaviest bombing in Britain.

As the taxi stopped in front of a dun-coloured apartment building, an elderly, thick-set man with a tweed cap pulled low over his forehead, came heavily down the steps followed by a busy Scots terrier.

"My father," Alistair said quietly and moved forward to greet him.

They spoke briefly then my father-in-law took my hand for a moment and I saw in his eyes something steady and good. "I'll be seeing you," he said, nodding; "Now I'll just take the wee dog for a walk."

I find it hard to write of the three weeks that followed, for it was as foreign a world to me as I was, as a person, to his parents.

꙳

"You'll be in your old room," my mother-in-law said to Alistair leading us into the apartment. "Tea at six in the kitchen." She nodded her head kindly at me "You'll be tired and wanting a wash and tidy up."

Alistair wandered about the room, touched a familiar cigarette burn on the dressing table, stopped to glance at a pen and ink sketch of Peebles where the family had once spent a holiday, then joined me at the window looking on to a quiet terrace.

"I think a drink is indicated, don't you?" I shook my head. Pulling a bottle of whisky from his gear he wandered off with it to his mother's kitchen for a glass, some water and possibly a chat.

He returned ruefully.

"What happened?"

"She said, 'And what would you be doing with a bottle of whisky in my house?'"

I laughed. "You'll probably be better without it." Together we went in for tea.

The large sitting room and dining room with its long mahogany table were no longer used. The friendly old-fashioned kitchen was the heart of the house. We sat at a table in front of a large black hearth, my father-in-law at the head with Alistair at his right. Alistair talking too fast, kaleidoscoping his war in Norway, and the quick withdrawal from there. Then the other war in Burma. Being taken prisoner at a jungle bivouac of the Japanese, and managing to escape. Then Rangoon to Calcutta via Northern Burma and Assam, where, wretchedly ill, he had finally been posted to

Ceylon. Watching, I noticed his father's concentration, the grey, balding head nodding occasionally. He asked brief, acute questions, with long intervals of listening, while his wife poured tea and piled our plates with delicious fried sole, a coming-home luxury in a deep post war economy.

❧

Anne, just eleven, settled remarkably well into life in Glasgow.

In the Wilson's flat in Burnbank Terrace where J.M.Barrie had once lived, she was happy delving into the many books that lay forgotten in their bookcases in the dining room. Dickens, Walter Scott, Jeoffrey Farnell, Huckleberry Finn, Tom Sawyer, Masterman Ready. It was quiet there, for the room had been abandoned since the beginning of the war. Here Anne sat quietly reading all day. When Alistair's father returned home and settled in his arm chair to read his newspapers, she would wangle her way to him gently, sit on the arm of his chair and tickle the soft white curls on the back of his head as she had done with Didi, her precious grandfather, my father. He would say little, for he was a quiet man and a child in the house rather surprised him, but there was an understanding between them closer than with any others of the family. He was a silent man but every now and then he would slip her a pound note, and it did our hearts good to see this strange bonding.

At night, through the long hours I listened to the separate chimes of Alistair's father's many clocks inexorably beating out the time.

Reality was Alistair and I making a go of what was now. *Please God, make it good.*

I had had no idea how strict rationing was, nor how few coupons were allowed for clothes and many other things. I did not realize till later, that my mother-in-law had had to queue for hours to get linen for us; that hot water was a preciously shared commodity until I had a glorious soak using the total output for the whole ménage. My offers to help were refused. In an effort to lessen the strain on that apartment, I walked one day in drenching rain and got bronchitis. Finding a suitable apartment was obviously a first priority.

It was difficult. Domestic help had been absorbed by the Services. Large houses too big to run without help were sold or converted into apartments, and quickly occupied. Happily, one of Alistair's two brothers managed to find an apartment for us that had just fallen vacant.

We stood in the greyness of a November afternoon in front of a green door awaiting an answer to our ring. A small woman with apple bright cheeks and a duster tied like a mop over her greying hair came to the door.

"Guid afternoon," she said in a strong Glasgow accent. "You'll be Mr. and Mrs. Wilson? Your brother told me to expect you."

"Mrs. Smith?"

"That's me,"

I liked her immediately. She had kind blue eyes, and her weatherworn face creased with her smile. "Och, come awa' in," she said. "It's a raw windy day for you to be standing out in it. And you from them Tropics and all! C'mon in, Hen!" she repeated holding her weatherworn hand out to me.

"What does 'Hen' mean?" I whispered to Alistair as we followed her inside.

"Dear," said Alistair.

There was a long central passage punctuated with doors on either side. She showed us the bedroom with a gas meter, a living room with a fireplace and bay windows. What was possibly the original kitchen had been subdivided by a half- frame forming two 10 x 12 ft. adjoining, open kitchens, each with a cooker, shelves and a table. Against the back wall of the passage was a large coalbunker, again halved for our neighbouring tenants and us. Sharing a kitchen would be interesting, I thought. The bathroom so far, remained a mystery.

"And this," said Mrs. Smith opening another door, "is the bathroom. Your bath nights will be Tuesdays and Fridays."

We walked out on the darkening pavements our breath smoky in the chill air.

"What did she mean, 'Bath nights Tuesdays and Fridays?'"

Alistair grinned. "There's a saying among Glaswegians that you don't want to rub the good grease off your body too often."

"But seriously?"

"It's not the end of the world. We'll get one of those light papier-mâché hipbaths. We'll fill a kettle or two of boiling water and there you are." said Alistair lightly. And he meant it. Already the Scots accent was heavier on his tongue. And so would be mine, they'd say, before we left Glasgow.

We moved into our new flat two days later.

≈

Our three-pounds-a week-apartment was central and people-friendly. I liked my brother and sister-in-law who lived in the adjoining apartment, and Mrs. MacLean the genteel District Nurse who was known as the Green Lady because of her green outfit. But I specially loved Mrs. Smith the caretaker, who lived in the basement with her dour husband. She was my confidante, my friend; I could cry on her shoulder, laugh with her, learn from her. She introduced me in turn to the butcher, the baker, the 'Jenny all sorts' shop, and the chemist.

It was she who helped sort out the complications of coupons, and what you could and could not do with them. Fats and meat were extremely highly rationed; dried eggs, which tasted of mould, replaced fresh eggs. Mrs. Smith told me how to make them edible; introduced me to thinly sliced Black sausages with dry-fried tomatoes; and advised that a shilling's worth of mince a week went much further than a 'cut' as it could be stretched with endless variations.

True, occasionally, a slender slice of meat could be available at an enormous price, but we had both determined that we would live within our limits - which was a low thirteen pounds a week, minus our three pounds a week for the apartment. So mince it was, or sausages made of heaven knew what, or a bit of fish, and once we had whale meat which look like liver and smelled of fish. One cold day at the height of winter our old butcher who always had a kindly word for me whispered, "You're lucky, Mrs. Wilson; I've kept a bonny piece for you today, and it's no more money either for you." It was well wrapped up and I hurried back happily. Unwrapping it at home I gazed into the sad, glazed eyes of a sheep's head, its teeth still green and grinning.

Almost falling I rushed down the curving stone stairs to the basement. "Mrs. Smith, oh, Mrs. Smith, I've got an awful thing to show you."

Standing arms akimbo with weather beaten hands over her aproned hips Mrs. Smith surveyed the beastie.

"Well I think if you'll excuse me saying so, Mrs. Wilson, I think you're awfu' fortunate, Hen," said Mrs. Smith still looking at it with pleasure.

"But its eyes, Oh Mrs. Smith what am I to do?"

She turned away for a moment, and with the flick of two thumbs there was my sheep shorn of its accusatory eyes.

It was, she said, at one time her job. She was twelve then, she added.

Everyone said how lucky I was, and that it would make a fine, rich broth. But I had none of it. I took it out finally onto icy pavements a foot deep with November's snow and put it on top of the garbage pail. For seventeen days its green teeth grinned at me during the garbage men's strike. It was said to be the worst winter in a hundred years.

Cooking had once been a fun thing for me. Now it became a challenge to feed my man appetizing food with what was available. My father wrote, "We were amused (amused! I could just see the chuckle widen his bony face) to read of your efforts at cooking.

Keep at it, Ducks! (What a horrible name for me!) Accept the challenge, as we know you can, and tell us more. I would love to try one of your dishes. Why not pep them up with a dash or two of chilli powder?" My mother wrote, "You say you can get milk and vegetables. Can you get cod liver oil, to take daily I mean, as a very necessary supplement against the cold weather? I have already sent you a bottle of *Cook's Joy*, which is all we can get now. I will send more soon. Darling, do wrap up warmly." The *Cook's Joy* - extracted from coconuts - nearly precipitated a crisis. The other occupants of the apartments complained bitterly about its odour. Would I please stop using it, or else.

Anne was remarkable. She settled in without a word as if these enormous changes were nothing. After going shopping with me once or twice, she was quick to say, "I can do it, Mum."

She learned to make her bed, fold her clothes, put them away, albeit a bit untidily. She, who had made such a fuss about eating in Ceylon, made no complaints about the strange, rationed food I produced.

We enrolled her in one of Glasgow's best day schools, Laurel Bank, and off she'd go in her green outfit. I'd watch her out of the tall windows in our living room, a small, gallant figure with slightly hunched shoulders, and my heart would go out to her. This was an Anne I'd never known. She was silent about her school. She, like me, was bad at maths; good at writing, history, geography and English.

One day Mrs. Smith came to me with her small face bruised and pinched with pain. She had fallen down the curving stone steps to her apartment, and had, apart from her face injuries, hurt her breast. Shyly she pulled apart her cheap blouse, her vest. The skin was badly bruised and reminded me of a friend who had had a similar injury long ago. Suddenly scared I suggested she went to the Glasgow Infirmary, not far from the apartment.

"Och! I'll nae go to tha' place, Mrs. Wulson! I won't at that!"

I suggested the Green Lady, or Mrs. Kerr, the lady downstairs with the blue striped milk jugs and who had the reputation of being a kleptomaniac. But Mrs. Smith would have none of them either.

"Och! No, Hen!" The scarf-wrapped head shook violently. A cold water compress, then? She said she could manage that, but still I worried for her, not quite knowing why.

One morning she showed it to me: A small, grey-blue lump in the cradle of her thumb and index finger.

"It's just a wee thing," Mrs. Smith said looking anxiously at me. "It dinna even hurt."

I cannot think what made the word 'Secondaries' flash into my mind. Perhaps some chip of overheard memory from my parents discussing a patient long ago.

Finally Mrs. Smith went into surgery. She had cancer of the breast. When I visited her in hospital she looked smaller than ever cocooned in her white hospital gown and bandages, but she was helping the nurses, taking tea, a careful cup at a time, to other patients. She greeted me with her old cheery smile "How are you, Hen? Och, I'm doing fine! They said they caught it in time. I'm ever so grateful to you." But I felt I should have persuaded her to go to the Infirmary earlier.

❧

Out of the blue, like a fairy godmother, Aunt Anna appeared. She was a dainty little person (my mother-in-law's sister) with a fluffy mass of white coiffeured curls, pink-rouged cheeks, and a wonderful sense of humour. She was warm and generous and I would think, in those early days, "Thank God for Aunt Anna!"

On her first visit to us she immediately took me in hand. "You'll be needing a warmer coat than that," she said fingering mine. "Good cloth, too. Pure wool, but it will NOT do for this weather. Not warm enough, and you coming all that way from India!"

"Ceylon," I said meekly.

"My cousin's husband said he couldn't stand the heat." She continued, then "Where did you get it?"

I didn't want to tell her that it had been made for me by the French couturier at *Cargills*, Colombo. "What about coupons?" I asked, instead, getting into the rhythm of the coupon thing.

"Don't you be worrying," she said, "Leave me to worry about that. I know an excellent furrier." She spoke in a precise way, her small mouth pursed a little. "It won't cost much."

I was relieved. Alistair had started working, and we just managed, with a little over. Yet it was clear that I needed warm clothes urgently.

Soon Aunt Anna, after taking me to a tiny shop in an unknown street, had me wearing a singularly unappealing, but warm 'mink marmot' coat in which I trotted around like some sort of mole. But she looked dainty as a small French doll in her black wool coat with a smart black fur collar. She always arrived unexpectedly, clutching in one black-gloved hand a bag of home-made jam or jelly, or a small bunch of whatever flowers were in season to hearten the day; the other hand holding against the wind a wildly angled hat to which she had added a touch of ribbon or net.

She was a wizard at getting the odd cashmere twin-set (in an 'Unsaleable colour,' so an absolute bargain 'and wonderful for you, dear,') or a skirt ('size 10, not a very popular size here, dear,') more or less coupon free. "It's helping trade," she said earnestly. It was helping me, too, who had not come with enough warm clothes. Once she had had a small boutique herself but what had happened to it no one knew.

❧

Then, Alistair's favourite cousins discovered us. Aunt Anna had spread the news. Two of them shopping in Glasgow had caught sight of Alistair and me in a bus and telephoned that evening.

I answered the telephone.

"Is that Alistair Wilson's house?" The accent, strongly Scottish, the voice, warm and excited. I said 'Yes.'

"Christine? Welcome to Glasgow! This is Flora. One of your new cousins!"

I quickly handed the telephone to Alistair. "My cousins the MacDonalds," he said after twenty minutes of excited chatter. "They've invited us for tea on Sunday." I had never heard of them. But he would tell me nothing.

All I knew of the Cousins was that Aunt Anna had been the closest link in the two families and she had given them our telephone number. They had all lost their husbands and lived together.

The bus travelled nearly an hour before we reached a pleasant suburb of Glasgow. Now as our steps echoed on the pavement of a quiet road hemmed with apartments, I drew my collar close against the whip-lash of the wind. Suddenly, past the blind eyes of endless curtained windows we came to a brightly lit bay window, with faces peering and hands waving. Before we could ring, the door burst open, and four girls poured onto the pavement to hug us and linking arms drew us into the warmth of the house. Inside, a beautifully furnished modern room with a blazing fire.

Cathy, stately and beautiful, was gracious and quiet. Helen, elegant with prematurely white upswept hair and classic profile, head of a smart department store. She would listen to arguments raging around her and enter with an authoritative summary that would quieten her sisters. Flora, the youngest, who wore charismatic blue eye shadow, changing hair styles and made passionate outcries about Scottish politics was the most demonstratively warm. Anne, monkey faced, quietly caring, did boutique style dressmaking and was to become my favourite, though I loved them all.

ALISTAIR PLUNGED WITHIN A few weeks of being in Glasgow into finishing his Engineering degrees at night classes. He had such an urgent need to get on with life, and catch up with his seven years in the army, that he had persuaded his College to allow him to take the four-year course in two. I saw his face grow wan, and watched him studying late into the night. Yet the humour was there, and the laughter and the gentleness. And the evening hours were empty when he was away.

I thought I had been settling rather well into our new life when there came from my father a sharply different letter from his usual ones. He was, apart from his surgical work, becoming increasingly absorbed in his studies of Ceylon's aborigines, the Veddas, and writing in depth about them. He was also deeply into Wild Life Preservation, and plunging, like a frail but valiant Don Quixote, into endless other causes. His letter flared into my perhaps too stagnant life and reminded me of other letters that had punctured various torpid areas of my being... "Good for you getting settled as you are doing. But what's happened to your writing? There you are in the heart of Scotland with learning facilities at your finger- tips. What are you doing about it?"

He and I were, for all our affection for each other, quick sparring partners. My instinct was to dash off an indignant letter. Where would I find time to write?

It was all very well for him! But of course he was right. I had known what it was to sit at my typewriter every morning and sharpen pencils, or stare at the aggressively empty sheet of paper in my small Smith Corona typewriter. On other days a flash of thought drove me to type, regardless of mistakes and that was the best way, at that time. In truth I had been wondering how to start writing again. The time was now.

It was by chance I found Mr. Scouller. A small magazine called *The Writer* started the search. After endless abortive phone calls I tried the Enquiries section of the *Glasgow Herald* and was told, "There is a Mr. Scouller who counsels a creative writers' group." I was given a telephone number.

"Edward Scouller." His voice is grating, strongly Glaswegian. Breaking into my stammering query, he asked, "Wilson? Would that be a Scottish Wilson?" I said, "Yes." We talked some more and he said, "Come along at six on Thursday and see for yourself what it's all about. We can talk more then. Right? Got the address? Aye, Bothwell Street, first floor, you'll find the door open."

❧

The room, which had been full of young voices, quietened as I entered. "Good God!" said Mr. Scouller, "So you're the girl with the English accent. And from wha' sunny part of the world did your Scottish husband find you?"

He was a small nut of a man in an old brown tweed jacket. Beneath a cap of thick grey hair his eyes shone bright as a bird's in his ruddy, seamed face. His twisted smile seemed slightly sardonic.

"Ceylon," I said.

"Ah, Ce-lon," then, turning to his class he said, "Christine Wilson - the Scouller Group. The lass has had work published."

"In Ceylon," I muttered.

"Furthermore," he added as if I had not spoken, "she wants - she would like - to be allowed to take the two year course in one year, God knows for what reason. Have you a reason?"

I looked at him. "No. But I'd like to try."

There were about thirty or forty students. Young men and women with bright, intelligent faces. Freckled faces among the girls and two or three flaming redheads. Tweeds. Plaids. Wool jackets hitched over the backs of chairs. The fug of stale cigarette smoke. The talk of students of writing, which I had never known.

Edward Scouller's classes were unique. Some years later glancing through a copy of *Readers Digest* I read an article about him. "Unknown except to very few," it began, "is a brilliant teacher in Glasgow, Scotland, where writers are taught to write…"

At the end of the class Scouller beckoned to me. Why did I wish to take the two-year course in one year? Was I so sure of myself? A note of near-hostility in his brusqueness threatened me.

I said, "I need to do it. Please."

He looked at me quizzically for a moment. "I'll take you up on that, Lassie, and I'll no' be sparing you. "Tuesdays and Fridays, then, and Thursday as well for the Scouller Group if you like. Bring something with you to show us what you can do."

I nervously handed him my manuscript.

There was a difference between my father's criticism of my work and Scouller's. My father slashed through what he thought was badly written; Edward Scouller used criticism like a scalpel, taught us how to suture the broken skin together.

He met Alistair and sometimes he invited us to have a drink with him at the Glasgow Press Club. I loved the smoke, the laughter, the swift, brilliant talk spiced with raw Scot.

There was one particularly icy day when he phoned me. "You've sent me a hell of a lot of stuff I can't possibly deal with in class. You'd better come and have a cup of tea with Mary and me on Friday so we can talk about it."

The snow lay thick as I had ever seen it, and still it snowed, driving across the windows of the bus that took me to Ibrox. It was a long journey. I was the last passenger on the bus when it set me down in what seemed a totally deserted area covered in whiteness. There was a blizzard blowing and I bent my head against its bite and felt my boots scrunch ice. Then I followed a trail of white-topped houses, and at last found Mr. Scouller's house.

Tobacco-stained teeth showing in a generous smile, a hand-knitted pullover, old slippers. He gestured towards a blazing fire, and we sat at the dining table littered with papers. Somewhere in the house his son played a highland lament on the recorder of the bagpipes.

"You'll have to decide," Edward Scouller said at last, "whether you write as I know you can, or get snarled up in the social life that awaits you."

In the weeks that followed I wrote and my pieces were read in that harsh grating voice of his. There would be criticisms and times when my manuscript came back slashed with red. "Is there a Christine Wilson dictionary?" "Tighten this up." "Clichés, clichés, clichés!" "Invest in a thesaurus." And, occasionally, "This is what I want." Suddenly I was part of a group with Tom who was a collier and wrote beautifully, Margaret, Fiona and Jim. After class, the five of us walked arm in arm down to a café where Alistair joined us after his class, and we'd sit talking until we were driven out into the cold Glasgow night.

෨

In the advanced class there was more specific reading, and more creative writing demanded. If my target for Mr. Scouller, of hopefully, one to two manuscripts a week, was demanding, Alistair's, with a large range of subjects necessary for his degree, was staggering. After returning from work he would study late into the night. But twice a week after his classes we still met 'The Group' for coffee, or occasionally Edward Scouller would invite us to the Glasgow Journalist's Club. Another Christmas went by; the end of our courses approached.

Alistair passed his exams with honours. I heard incredulously that I had won a first and a second award in the two-in-one course I had taken.

IN THE SPRING OF the next year we moved into a small house of our own. At the end of a row of similar small houses built on the site of a large bombed area, it faced a pleasant park, and had a promising garden.

Below the hill on which Dalmuir stood, stretched the vast expanse of the Clyde where the bombing had been most extensive. Much of it still remained derelict with the spare masts of ships standing tall against a dour sky, and the collieries, silent. This was Clydebank, 1947.

Here men in dark clothes with caps pulled low over their foreheads slouched along the pavements. Women in headscarves pushed prams loaded - apart from a baby or two - with careful shopping. At the butcher's they thrust forward ration books for the inevitable weekly shilling's worth of meat, or whatever was going cheaply. On one occasion I saw wealthy people buying expensive cuts of meat that the butcher was only too ready to sell in a non-buyer's market, and heard the anger of the people. Then the shouting ceased almost as abruptly as it had begun, and they moved on silently to pick over bargain vegetables: turnips, kale, cabbage, the best value for money, and a 7 lb bag of 'tatties'. Sometimes through the drab crowd a girl would swing past with lipstick bright as a poppy's, high heels mocking the rain, and a swirl of her skirt.

I followed the pattern; bought my 7 lb. bag of potatoes and lugged it up the hill to our house. I learned not to smile at people as I always had, as it was sometimes misunderstood. You could either be daft, or wanton; nor was hanging out the washing on a Sunday tolerated, as Alistair gently told me. I learned also that there were two disparate kinds of people living in our area. Those of Dalmuir and Clydebank: each with its own codes and mores. Brought up to recognize no difference between people I was at first lonely for the easy friendliness of the Glasgow apartment and drew closer into writing.

We bought a small inexpensive car, and began to explore at weekends Scotland's glens and lochs, its scattered castles and islands. One day we decided to visit Loch Ness in the North-West Highlands. The newspapers had been full of the story of the mythical monster of the Loch, whose depths were said to be uncharted. Those who claimed to have seen it were explicit. The majority, who did not, lampooned it mercilessly.

On a bright summer's day we left Glasgow, passed moor lands where Angus cattle grazed, and hedgerows cascaded wild blackberries; then away to the North and West past dour glens and moors, in rising country till we were in the silence of the highlands. The road was quiet, with hills rising sheer, and valleys immensely deep, set with craggy boulders. I heard a mountain eagle cry and saw it soaring high above the lonely glen. Far below us between the Moray Firth in the North opening into the North Sea, and the Firth of Lorn opening into the Atlantic Ocean in the West, winds Loch Ness, cutting a sword-swathe into the upper third of Scotland through a narrow cleft in the mountains. We stopped then breathing in the thin, cold air and jumped out of the car and on impulse I plunged my hands into the heather and found at last the white heather I sought for good luck.

The sun had disappeared when we reached the loch side, and heavy cloud hung over a sheet of pewter water. We stopped by an inlet where the loch scooped deeply into a rocky trough of water. There was a strange silence about the land. Not a bird sang, though there were trees; nothing moved. Not even the merest ripple stirred that grey slate of water.

Alistair set the car in gear and we began to move away. "No monster. Bad luck," he said cheerfully. One can imagine anything in this place. I stared at the depthless water. Nothing. Far out to the left I saw a growing ripple, and then another, further along. And another. Then as slowly as they appeared the ripples receded.

"What are you looking at?" Alistair asked amused. "The monster?"

"No," I answered. "Nothing."

❧

I realised a long time ago that Alistair was special.

It took a strong man to marry someone not only five years older than himself but who came of a blend of East and West of which I was proud; while he came of an equally proud Scottish family, one of whom had no wish to step across the Scottish-English border.

More than that, I was not a competent person, never would be. I dreamed dreams, painted, saw stories in clouds, wrote, joined endless courses in all the things that interested me, and somehow in the balance it worked out. Sometimes things went wrong but they were worked out, too.

It was there I began to call him 'Guardie'. In addition there was my daughter, Anne, who loved him dearly, and fitted snugly into the vastly different circumstances in which we now lived. She liked her excellent day-school, Laurel Bank, showed sudden interest in cooking, with the provisory, "Don't tell me how, Mummy. The books will tell me," loved listening to "Just William!" and "Dick

Barton!" on radio, and was as happy as I had ever seen her. When, my parents arrived in London my father's first call was to her.

That she missed Ceylon, her grandparents, the dogs, was understandable. But she had adapted amazingly well.

❧

My parents came to visit us. In 1948 plane flights to London involved overnight stops at Bahrain and Karachi. But they decided they would come by sea.

I met them in London. They looked well, my mother, a little thinner. They had made an appointment to see a specialist in London about her thyroid. My father, skeletal thin as always, but in holiday mood, bought an atrocious checked tweed coat 'for the cold of Scotland.' My mother was eager to unpack the presents she had brought.

Three days later they came up on the day train to Glasgow. How was the thyroid test, I asked. Not too bad, they said, it required a small operation, which could be done later.

I still worried about my mother's tiredness when they joined us in Glasgow. After an early supper I promised her breakfast in bed. That night she went into a major stroke. No speech. No movement. Life only in beseeching eyes.

"What are we to do?" I asked helplessly.

My father said nothing.

❧

Somehow the news of my mother's stroke got around our small circle of friends. They were there, backing us, quietly. A yet-unknown neighbour dropped by one day to offer two eggs in a little basket. "We are sorry to hear about your mother," she said shyly. "I was lucky to get two fresh eggs this morning. Maybe your mother would like them?" and a friendship was born that day.

The hospital did not allow food to be brought in, I told her, but she insisted, "Och, it's nothing. You look as if you could use them yourself, and your puir, thin father." After she'd gone I looked at them, and my hand shook. It was months since I had touched a real egg. What would I make with these to make the most of them for my two men, my husband and my father, and my daughter brought home from school for her first holidays.

Mr. Scouller phoned. "Bring your father to our next meeting," he said.

The two men met. Two scholars brought together by tragedy. Their hands gripped. There was no need for words. Mr. Scouller began his discourse that evening with his typical grin, "This is the first time I have had the pleasure of having two generations of writers at one of my meetings." Then quietly went on with the meeting. My father enjoyed every moment of it. Afterwards the two men talked quietly, and as we went home to Dalmuir he said, "You're lucky, Bunting. He's a fine man."

The cousins phoned often. One day they asked diffidently, "This is a bad time, but we would be happy if you would bring your father to tea on Sunday."

My father's face lit with pleasure. He had heard so much about the cousins, he said.

They asked him about the jungles and once more his eyes brightened with memory.

That night he held them entranced with his stories of jungles, and jungle people. Watching them sitting on the edge of their chairs, Anna with her hands clasped on her lap; Flora leaning forwards slightly, chin in cupped hands; Cathy erect in her chair like some princess; Helen, attentive, assessing, I listened to a story I remembered.

"I was walking through the jungle," he said, "and suddenly I saw a remarkable sight. There in front of me was an antlered sambhur with its hind quarters suspended in mid air –"

"Oh!" breathed Anna, her grey eyes wide. The others sat mesmerized.

"But that was not all," he continued. "On the branch above was a great python with wide open jaws sucking it up." He looked at each of his listeners in turn.

"And then," he said, "I passed my hand between them… and the sambhur ran away into the jungle. Broke the magnetism, you see."

There was silence for a moment, then Helen said, "He's pulling our legs."

It was good to hear my father laugh again. He went away promising to return and they each in turn hugged him. "Take care," they said, and to me, "He's a grand person."

"You're in our thoughts. Take care."

"You're lucky to know them, Bunting," my father said as we went home.

❧

As I sit writing this, so many years later, I recall that I never did find people quite their like again. Straight, decent, warm-hearted, they gave, asking nothing in return. But they did more than that, physically. Helen, head of a department store, said, "Come over," and in those difficult days of post- war Britain helped me refit myself for the chill of Scotland for I had nothing usable. Anne made my first outfit for a BBC interview, and to meet my parents when I went up to London. They gave me ration-time recipes, advised, comforted. One or other would phone daily or I would phone them.

Sometimes Alistair and I took risks on the restless streets of that post-war, uneasy Glasgow, leaving Anne and her grandfather to chat together. I open my diary at random.

Last night we went to a restaurant that had just opened. Situated in the midst of Glasgow's worst slums, in a street of razor-slashers, pimps and juvenile delinquents, it is reached down cobbled alley-ways at the back of a tough drinking pub.

Louts and layabouts lean against doorways and street lamps in small groups, legs crossed, cigarettes drooping from the corner of their lips, eyes slanting to view 'the toffs' who draw up in their big cars. A striped alley cat slinks along the gutter. An old man, stubble like hoar frost crusting his sunken cheeks, shuffles off in a thrown-out overcoat into the gloom of the wintry night.

The men stand watching; silent, contemptuous. Those bound for the restaurant that offers the best of food in the middle of a slum, hurry in, for there is something uncomfortable about these pavements.

Inside, bottles of Chianti hang like clusters of grapes from the beam above the bar. There is pâté maison, melon and prosciuto, roast leg of lamb for the people inside; pork for the hard-faced, whisky-husky wine buyer from London, while his wife waits at home. ("I'll be a bit late home from office, dear.") A prostitute sits at the bar and steadily drinks her whisky. She is young, this one, her hair, bleached silver white, puffed high like a dandelion clock, her eyes expressionless.

And outside, the men of the street watch.

Another night, after lectures we had to walk home in the dark taking a short cut through the Botanic Gardens. There was no one there; just the two of us, the hollow resonance of our feet, and the eerie feeling that someone was following us. Nothing to see, but a presence to feel and a different kind of chill making me reach for my husband's arm.

"Is there someone there?" I ask.

"Can't see anyone."

"What do we do?"

"Walk."

Then at last we are out of 'the place.'

"Alistair, I swear I heard footsteps following. No echo, just steps."

He is looking at me, a funny look on his face. "A memory of steps, perhaps. People have been murdered there on deeply foggy nights. Fog like that can do strange things to people."

THE INFIRMARY TO WHICH my mother was rushed was unable to keep long-term patients. What next? "Back home!" My father said incisively. Always skeletal thin he was drowned in a vast checked jacket from which his angular face jutted defiantly.

How complicated it was that late summer of 1948 to get my mother moved anywhere. Flights took longer and made almost impossible stipulations. To travel by rail to London a specially reserved compartment and a nurse were mandatory. But there were no nurses available at the time. Finally, because my mother had been Chairperson of the Ceylon Red Cross Society during the war, a lovely lady of the Glasgow branch volunteered. My father's face is ashen. His lips a thin line.

I stand on the platform facing the open door of the carriage. I have no words, for what can I say. The great engine breathes a final gust of acrid smoke and almost silently the train moves. Alistair stands by me, his grip tightening on my hand.

My father's grief was frightening. He would not speak of Clarie and grew silent when we did. One evening he walked alone over the scary moors that rose above Dalmuir, his hands thrust deep in his raincoat pockets. The moors were notorious for its criminals but he did not care. Twilight was darkening when he returned, with two doubtful looking figures disappearing in the gloom behind him.

"I lost my way," he said, simply. The men had appeared out of the mist and he had asked for help. As they walked back together over the moors he asked what work they do for a living, and they said, "Nothing."

What *did* they do? Work in the shipyard in Clydebank. But they were laid off. It was hard on the bairns, but they managed. They asked what he did, and he told them about jungles and jungle people, and they asked for more. They brought him to our gate and took off their caps as he held out his hand to them in friendship. Then with a quick nod they were off into the shadowed road before they could be offered the insolence of money.

જ

I rushed down from Glasgow one weekend to visit my parents in London. Incredibly my father had found an Anglican hospice for Clarie in the East End of London. A surgeon friend had recommended it as a gentle place where she could be while they awaited a passage back to Ceylon. There, monks in brown habits, tonsured heads and sandaled feet, moved silently, arms crossed inside their cassock sleeves. No raucous sound of traffic intruded. It was a shabby building but mother's tiny room was immaculate, and she was cared for with efficiency and tenderness. More importantly, there was a spartan room with board for my father. It was the perfect haven for two deeply wounded people. In the quiet corridors the monks moved silently in shabby robes and sandaled feet, and there was the murmured hum of prayer. Here my mother lost her tortured look and lay without weeping. Her silver hair, still beautiful, softened her sunken cheeks. My father, for once not restless, sat by her and said to me quietly, later, "Without her I would be nothing."

જ

Too many things happened to us that high summer of sunshine, with the beauty of Scotland suddenly overwhelming because we were going to leave it, and I realised that I had learned to love it.

Alistair had achieved his degree, and was told that telescoping his four-year degree course into two years as he had done would never be allowed again. My success at Edward Scouller's class encouraged me. The pace of work had left us both restless, and when it was over we were bereft.

We badly missed our classes, the friendships and the chatter of intelligent young people. Sometimes at evening I heard Alistair talking to himself in a low rumble in the attic where he took refuge, while I fretted uselessly downstairs. But at weekends we drove deep into the country of the lochs and castles and made wild plans about going to South America or any country except, strangely enough, my island, which had in this year of 1948 gained it's Independence and was now called by its ancient name, Sri Lanka. That decision had to be my husband's however much I longed for it.

Alistair loved Ceylon, too. Unknown to me he wrote to the head of Colombo's largest engineering firm enclosing his curriculum vitae. Three weeks later he was asked to visit the firm's London office. He asked for one day's leave, took a night train, kept his appointment, returned on the night train and was in his father's office next morning. He had been accepted, but would have to spend six weeks with certain UK engineering companies represented by the team in Ceylon. It was going to be hard telling his father that he would be leaving.

When Alex Wilson, Alistair's father heard the news he turned heavily to a friend who had just walked into the house.

"What d'you think of this, Tom? My son's got a job in Ceylon."

"That's great news, Alex," was the reply. "What's the pay like?"

"Good. Very good. That's it then, son."

My father-in-law was a quiet man who took things in his stride, but was obviously proud of his son. The family, and in particular my mother-in-law, would miss him. She and I had developed a mutual respect and affection for each other specially after, unknown to me at first, she had visited my mother on her own a number of times in the Glasgow Infirmary and the two of them had managed to communicate in some strange language of their own. "She knew who I was," she told me. "Her mind understands. A lovely person."

Alistair departed for his visits in England. There were things to be sorted and packed in our home. Every event seemed to carry a new nostalgia. The chats with the cousins and Aunt Anna tightened. My phone calls to Mr. Scouller, who had become my mentor, philosopher, and friend, grew more urgent. "Just go ahead and write," he said with more gruffness than usual at our last meeting.

Anne leaves for Cheltenhan. We are miserable

Anne who had been with us through all our time in Glasgow was accepted at Cheltenham, my mother's school. The three of us were very close and the parting was hard. But it was arranged that she flew out for holidays with us. After she passed her school-leaving certificate rather brilliantly at 15, she went on to Château Brillamont in Lausanne to study French.

Alistair through all these ordeals was a tower of strength, amazing in a still-young man who knew nothing of such emergencies. He had phoned doctors, seen to the practical side of everything, been accepted for an engineering appointment in Ceylon, and, after a short special course, returned to fly out with me to Ceylon, leaving my parents in London to follow by sea with a trained nurse, when they could find one. Part of our hearts, our youth, would be left with 'Halcyon,' the small house where we had been so happy.

WHEN WE ARRIVED IN Sri Lanka, Suppiah, my father's Tamil driver, met us, his bone thin face rigidly emotionless, a shine of welcome in his eyes.

My throat tightens as we pass familiar sights: mangy dogs and scraggy cattle rooting garbage; a garish funeral parlour; boutiques bright with plastic toys; and finally a road with endless bicycle repair shops. Malligawatte - I had driven through it all so often.

Alistair too is bright with remembrance of his army days here. Pointing to places once filled with troops. Telling me about places as if he were telling a stranger; he spoke about these landmarks of his own during his four years on the island during the war.

On the polished cement veranda of Wycherley there is no one to greet us. Suppiah had forgotten to sound his horn at the gate, and while he hurriedly rings the bell we are already in the hall and Elvira, our beloved matron of the nursing home comes through to meet us, her pale, Italian face full of grief as she embraces us.

Two months later my father brought my mother back by sea with a trained nurse.

֍

"These are for you," my father said when he brought my mother home to Wycherley, and placed in my hand a string of pearls she had worn the day she and my father arrived in Glasgow from London. She seldom wore them, for every time she did, she said, there was a death in the family. They lay in my palm, warm as if they had come fresh-worn on her throat, incandescent, the nacre softly rose.

We had bought them together long ago. When I was just turning twelve, and about to be confirmed at our Anglican Church, St. Michael's, my father came into the bedroom to say good night, and asked what I would like as a confirmation present. "Anything?" I asked.

"Anything," he replied.

"A string of pearls for Mummy," I said.

৵

I remembered trips that Alistair and I had taken with my father. Today a weathered old Land Rover lies in a distant garage. Next to it is a trailer fitted to specifications provided by Alistair and my father. Hitched to the Land Rover, it jauntily followed us anywhere we wished; stumbled in and out of potholes, bounced, trotted, danced after us into some of the loneliest places in Sri Lanka, and made it possible for us to camp wherever and whenever the mood suited us. Before its arrival we sometimes camped on the veranda of an empty village school, a half-walled building, with a few desks and chairs inside. More than once I awoke to see small, astonished faces gazing at me. Once we tried crossing a river deeper than we thought and sank, water lapping the doors, and we marooned inside, with not a person in sight in heavy elephant jungles. Then suddenly, a band of men with heavy coils of rope broke through the forest cover and marched towards us.

They looked tough men, on a nefarious job for which they could have been imprisoned. But my father had immediate rapport with jungle people.

"Ah! Elephant noosers!" he cried, delighted. "See their deer-hide ropes!"

A few words of greeting, and soon they were pulling us back on land, and chatting with us. What were we doing here? Why had we come? They had heard of the Dosthera Mahatmaya (Doctor).

My father spoke happily with them as if they were well-known friends, asked where they came from, how they went about their illicit capturing of elephant, for he was genuinely interested. He had a disarming way about him that made people – whoever they were – talk easily. We left at last, and my father sat back in his seat silent, absorbed in thought.

"You're going to write about them, of course," I asked.

"Of course. These are people whose lands are being destroyed by elephants. The only answer is to set forested areas aside as corridors for elephants to move from one jungle to another in the drought as they do in Africa. It makes this sort of thing inevitable." These villagers, too, had problems with their crops constantly being raided.

He once worked tirelessly to organize the people of a village to drive an isolated herd of elephants suffering badly from drought to greener forests. When the day arrived, a threadbare drizzle fell, and only a few people straggled in without enthusiasm for the Great Elephant Drive. The whole exciting venture failed miserably. "It is the God's will," they muttered sullenly returning to their villages, leaving a saddened old man who had tried and failed.

In the weeks following my parents' return Alistair and I watched my father with concern. Now he seemed demon-driven, operating, seeing patients, lecturing, writing his books as if he must drown thought. And every day, twice a day, the hardest thing of all, he visited my mother in the small nursing home adjoining the house. "Your mother loved my poems," he said abruptly, "I was thinking about those pearls from our now-ruined pearl banks. Do you remember, Bunting, when we sailed there, long ago, when we travelled the sea route to Wilpattu?" Then, surprisingly, "Why don't you and Alistair take a break? Take the Land Rover; visit the beaches of the forgotten fisheries. There's nothing there now but sea and sand, but it will do you good, and find for me, if you can, an old ruin I've always wanted to visit. They call it the Doric, at Arippu."

Alistair and I, had read of the strange old building the British had built to entertain top officials and important visitors to the fisheries, and thought it intriguing, so one long weekend we took my father's suggestion, packed our camp beds and bedding, enough to eat, and set out to find the Doric.

འ

We drove to a lonely spur of land on the west coast, to Kalpitiya, found a deserted beach, and camped in derelict Police quarters that had formerly guarded the pearl banks. That evening we walked on a beach fretted with the shimmer of pearl oyster shells, our bare feet crunching sand ground with millenniums of them. Stooping, I let it drift through my fingers and taking my husband's hand in mine, said, "Look, my love," and poured silvered sand through his fingers. There was a lift in the breeze, a song in the sea, and no one but us.

We swam, and that evening walked the beach in search of the Doric, but did not find it. Again next day we searched, until the sun burned the sand under our feet, too hot to bear. Perhaps it no longer existed? The winds were strong; monsoons beat heavily on that coast. But that evening as we walked further, it loomed before us, a lonely ruin on a forgotten shore. A vision arose in my mind of this place in the days of The Fisheries when the masts of

Alistair and I camping, 1948

many ships from many lands rode the sea, and ashore, Pearl Town had arisen almost over night, a palm-hatched shanty town overrun with people, boutiques, lodgings. People of many races thronged boutique-lined roads foetid with the stench of rotting oysters. Merchants, visitors from across the seas, ladies with parasols and lace handkerchiefs held to delicate nostrils, murderers creeping at night beyond the flare of torches, a sudden scream – the rush of footsteps. At dawn the cry of jungle fowl in the encroaching forest.

Long after they had gone, the forgotten Doric remained. Ruin though it was, it stood proud against the sky. Balls had been held there. Up the curving, cemented stairs gloved guests with fans, in nineteenth century evening dress climbed to dine and dance under the moon.

Now, its broken walls stood stark against an evening sky, a rare Black Eagle on its crumbling summit. Only part of the double stairway remained, and the moonlit shore. It was not the first time I had visited, in a different time, that magic pearl country, for a different reason.

∾

My mother died quietly in the Wycherley nursing home after four years of silence. Yet I know with absolute certainty that though the only word she could utter was "No," which meant all things, she had more comprehension than anyone guessed. One day I set the typescript of my first book on a reading stand in front of her open at page 1, the rest dog-eared for easy turning. Quietly I told her what it was about, and taking her 'good' hand showed how easily she could turn a page. Later, it had been turned to page three; and every day another page or two had been turned until the end, when all she could say was a quiet "no," of approval, her fingers curling over mine. Only once during her long illness did she, incredibly, speak. Knowing how much she had loved dogs I went to her bedside one morning with a small golden spaniel puppy I had been given. Immediately the words burst out of her, "How… sweet!" I ran to tell everyone, but she never spoke again.

ENCOURAGED BY EDWARD SCOULLER, I had begun to write and be published. "Don't worry about not having an outlet for your short stories," he had written, "Just keep writing, that's the important thing. You say you don't know enough about your island (which seems strange to me, having met your father). Start to know it. A little research won't do you any harm. Be eclectic; though you are, unfortunately, a fairly delicately brought up creature, apart from your torrid journeys into the jungles, plunge into whatever subject comes your way."

One day my friend, Ryan, the brilliant, rather unorthodox young lay priest I had known a long time ago, visited. "You're writing a lot," he said to me, "but you haven't touched the realities of life. I could tell you enough to fill several books but it wouldn't be your kind of subject." He loved to provoke me.

"Such as…?"

"The kind of prostitution that's going on here." He spoke soberly.

"Ryan. I do care. What are you trying to tell me?"

He looked at me thoughtfully, "You've changed a lot. What did Glasgow teach you? Maybe you could write something. Look, I'll come round tomorrow morning if you feel like looking at the fringe of what's happening under the skin of 'respectable' Colombo."

"I'll take you up on your challenge. Whatever it is, let's go for it."

He called for me in his shabby bug Fiat. "What you are going to see is probably not what you expected. I'm going to show you the other side of prostitution."

We drove silently past the glossy area of Colombo to a sleazy suburb where a clutter of shabby dwellings leaned against each other and litter smeared the pavements. Turning into a lane, we stopped before a small, neat house. "She's expecting us," he said. "Just watch and don't make small talk."

The door was instantly opened by a pretty woman in her thirties. Her pale olive face warmed as she saw Ryan, and as she backed against the open door to let us in, I noticed her heavy eyes. The room was almost clinically neat. In the angle of two walls behind a glowing red candle, stood a small statue of the Virgin Mary.

She gestured us to chairs, and in a moment brought a shiny metal tray set with a bottle of lemonade and two glasses. "Please!" she said, carefully filling the glasses. Ryan set down his glass and the two of them moved away quietly to talk.

I sat taking it in. The clapboard house in a squalid district; this room, immaculately clean. Five upright chairs loosely circling a small square table. A closed door. Again I look at the Madonna, her porcelain smile set in eternal forgiveness. The woman's hands move evocatively as she speaks with Ryan, but I cannot hear what she is saying. Her hair mahogany, with a touch of chestnut ripples over her shoulders with her movements. She wears no make up, not even lipstick. She is still beautiful, this woman in the startling fuchsia-pink silk dressing gown.

Ryan rose. I rose as well, and thanked her for the lemonade. She stood before him with her hands pressed over her breast, her head bowed as he murmured a blessing, and I heard her whispered, 'God Bless you,' as we left.

"She's Italian," Ryan said as we drove away. "The only way I could have you meet her was by saying you wanted to adopt a baby."

"A baby!!"

"God forgive me! There are plenty of those around! Not hers. She'd been so brutally raped she could never have a child. But she knows where they are available - for adoption, better homes, she hopes."

He told me she had married a Singhalese soldier in Italy during the war when she was sixteen. He brought her here where she was not accepted. He deserted her and prostitution became the only way she could make a living. "She's one of the top Madames," he said quietly. "She's also surprisingly enough an ardent Catholic and gives a lot to the church." He looked sardonically at me. "That's not one of the reasons I try to help her. She's tried to commit suicide several times. She needs help."

"But you don't mind accepting her money for your church?" Ryan stared at me. "Mea Culpa…! I get angry when I see her but…"

More quietly he continued, "She's a Catholic. Why shouldn't her money be accepted? It's the only way she feels she can atone. If it was refused she would have committed the greater sin of taking her life. She's tried often enough, God knows."

"But you're not Catholic." As a lay priest he wore grey trousers and a white open-necked shirt.

"She trusts me because I visit this area. It's part of my Parish. You, in your plush life, couldn't begin to dream what she's been through. Want to be driven home now?"

I shook my head. Inside I hurt. We drove on, but the sick feeling kept churning in my stomach.

≈

In the next house two dazzlingly pretty Burgher girls, fair-skinned, young. One with a baby nestling in her arms came forward. She was, I learned, sixteen.

They cried out happily like children and waved as they saw Ryan, "Hi, Ryan, come in Ryan. See how baby's growing!"

"This is the lady I told you about."

They smiled and nodded, and I held out a finger to the baby who gripped it tightly and the choked feeling in my throat grew. Then words came, and suddenly I was talking with them. They took me into a bedroom with a baby's cot decked in dotted muslin and pink satin bows; once more I drank lemonade served on a fancy tray. Again there was quiet talk with Ryan. Before we left a young macho lout swaggered in wearing a red cotton vest and a visored cap worn backwards. "Hi!" he said raising one hand. He put his arms round the two girls, and said, "Very pretty girls, no?" And when we left, "See yar," mockingly.

The sisters were sixteen and eighteen. The man, the husband of the older one, 'hired' them out. The baby was available for adoption in a better home than they could offer. Ryan said Mariella's message was that she had found a good home for the baby.

∻

The next house was furnished with maroon velvet cushions, upholstery and curtains. In it, incongruously, was an expensive sewing machine. The woman, Ryan said quietly, was the queen bee of them all. "She calls the deal for all the others in her web. A mercilessly evil woman."

She glided in silently on high, stiletto heels, as well dressed, as quietly spoken, as any friend of my mother's. She poured sherry for us, and it was she who led the conversation, speaking in a taut cultured voice of the recent races.

"Ryan, darling, I must tell you," she cried. "I won a thousand rupees at the Races on Governor's Cup day! Wasn't that mah-vell-ous!"

"I saw Mariella today," Ryan said soberly.

Her face changed. "She's mad!" she said harshly. "She came to see me yesterday. I told her to get the hell out of here."

"Don't try any of your tricks with her," Ryan said, in a voice I had never heard before. The next moment she was simpering, falsely genteel again, offering more sherry.

"Mariella's going straight, she told me." Ryan said.

Her heavily made-up face cracked in a smile. "What? Her? She's addicted."

I saw a small pulse beat in Ryan's throat.

"And who gives her the stuff?"

"Bullshit, Ryan! Where the hell did you get that story? Look, I'm sorry, but I have a woman coming for a fitting now. My client will be here any moment. So nice to have seen you both."

Abruptly a door snapped shut behind us.

"She sells Mariella dope," Ryan said. "Heroin."

"I think I'd like to go home," I said. All the way home I kept remembering the sad, heavy eyes of Mariella, and another picture of a twelve year old Tamil girl asleep on a rush mat in a hut with a wizened white baby crying beside her.

ALISTAIR PLUNGED ENTHUSIASTICALLY INTO his new work, challenged by the knowledge that the policy of his firm was to update it into the finest agro-engineering company in the island. Its buildings, scattered over a large area of land facing Beira Lake, thrummed with the beat of heavy engines and had a workforce of about fifteen hundred. What lay ahead required tact, for its all-British, predominantly Scottish heads of departments and managerial staff had been there a long time.

Dressed in new white shorts, a new open-neck shirt and a new hair-cut he came to be inspected.

"Alright?"

I hugged him. "Great. Good luck, Sweetie."

From our sitting room upstairs I stared at the tops of three houses across the way where the graphite mine had been.

Time to get down to writing. Time enough and to spare for that, and yet not the heart to do it. Friends to see, and yet I didn't want to see anyone.

I wandered down to the nursing-home to chat with Vera the matron, who sat in her white muslin hood and white uniform scribbling diets on a slate with a graphite pencil.

One hand on her shoulder, I stared down at the neatly written list. My mother used to do that, with that slate.

"We miss her, don't we?"

She put down her stylus. "We're praying all the time for them both."

"I can't pray. Why, Vera, why? Dear Lord, let her be well — what are the right words?"

"Sometimes there's no need for words," she said. Her face, grown old, was very beautiful. "Help me, Auntie Vera, help me." I said, quoting words I had used very long ago. Then switching subjects rapidly. "I must write. Write! It's the only way. Or is it?"

"It could be."

That day I went to my desk and began to type — something.

At first there seemed to be little for me to do at Wycherley. My father had long ago worked out a time-schedule, beginning with morning tea, and ending with a gong to announce dinner at 7.45pm, precisely. It was charted in my mother's handwriting. My job, as hers had been, was to see that everything was efficiently done as it always had been.

Upstairs in her mist-blue sitting room with blue chintz roses, her presence was strongest. On her desk was a small silver-framed picture of a baby who had just learned to sit. Here my mother had sat when she wasn't writing special diets for patients, answering the telephone, writing endless letters for my father, and reading a book a day, while totally out of character, she smoked through a tin of cigarettes.

I often sat in her chair, aware of the frail scent of *Quelques Fleurs* toilet water, contradicted by the lingering tobacco smell. Why had no one tried to stop her smoking? "Why, Daddy, why?" I asked my father. He had answered frowning, "She started after Yvonne's death. Do you think I didn't try to get her out of that damnable habit?" He broke off abruptly, then, very quietly added, "Better that, than…" and said no more.

Long ago, before I went away to school, my mother and I had talked of her school in England, and how happy she had been there. Of an evening she would sit fanned by a quiet breeze blowing the fragrance of an orris root fan on the balcony, her prematurely silvered hair set in neat waves over a wide forehead, her only concession to fashion. In her wardrobe, dresses with Paris and London labels hung unworn, and my father's voice, "Why don't you wear them, Clarie, instead of the cottons and flowered prints you wear? Why do you wear a necklace of beads, when I have given you a diamond and yellow sapphire pendant, clear as the finest whisky? Or the pearl necklace from the oysters of Ceylon?"

I'd sit on a footstool at her feet, one arm over her knees, and we'd talk about her school in England, her time as a medical student, her concern for my frail but indomitable father or some trivial problem of my own. Strange, for though I found it easier to confide in my father, so many others came to seek her advice as a physician and friend. I'd remember how she called me 'darling' in an impersonal way, a stray finger perhaps smoothing a wayward curl on my forehead, and suddenly her absence was unbearable and all I could do to drown the lost years of her was to write, write, while she lay immobile.

~

I wrote steadily to the newspapers, radio, random stories, plays. But at the back of my mind an embryo thought had begun to crystallize. The memory of the abandoned coffee estate near *Herondale.*

But first I had to learn intimately my island's history. There was a mass of knowledge available in my father's library, but at the Colombo Museum I found a fantastic library and a librarian - Lyn Fonseka. By special permission I was allowed to type my notes in a private section of his office. I, whose reports in England at school invariably read, 'Christine is always looking out of the window,' was suddenly insatiable for knowledge.

"Lyn, tell me, have you anything on the language our elephant trainers use?" I was writing a trio of articles on the capture and training of wild elephants. Lyn produced the information. Whatever material I needed he found. The British colonialists had left a treasure trove of published material about the island, as had the Dutch, and the Portuguese before them.

My files, typed on half sheets of typing paper, kept in alphabetical order in a shoebox, grew until it bulged with notes ranging from Anuradhapura to Zeilan - the old Dutch name of the island. Library research ran concurrent with intensive exploratory trips with my father, and when possible, with Alistair.

⁊

We had settled well into our life in Colombo with Alistair now chairman of his company, when a letter arrived inviting my father, Alistair and me to spend a weekend with an - unknown to us - planter friend of my father's.

"Why don't you two go? I can't get away." We hesitated as we didn't know him.

"Go!" he said. "You're lucky. Not many people are invited to Killarney now. And don't forget to ask him about the Devil Bird."

He pointed with his pipe towards a bookcase. On top was a spectacularly mounted bird with hooked talons, a four-foot spread of wings and a wide, open beak that screamed voicelessly. I had heard its cry once in the Pollebedde jungles. An eerie sound, rising in a long-drawn-out shriek that cut out abruptly. A bird of ill omen, they said. Its identity is still disputed.

"You're always talking about the Pioneers," said my father. "He's one of the last of them."

⁊

We drove towards the hills, snaking along sharply rising bends with glimpses of far, blue-hazed mountains. On one side, the road clung to the hillside; on the other it dropped sheer, three hundred feet and more, into deep ravines. A long time ago the car in which I travelled skidded over the edge on a similar road and I was saved, 18 feet down, by a single dadap tree.

The road climbed till the air grew thin and our breath hazed the windshield. We turned off at a dispensary into an estate road lined with fat green tea bushes, and beyond, the rich hills and valleys of the estate.

Unexpectedly, we entered a forest of lichened trees and wild rhododendrons. Everywhere in that moist, shadowy wilderness red anthuriums grew tall and orchids dripped splashes of colour. Abruptly the forest opened and we stopped before a stone-built bungalow.

White-haired, with wind-reddened cheeks, and wearing a green, Old School blazer, our host Douglas Kelly hurries to greet us as fast as his ebony cane allows. A razor nick covered with a fleck of cotton wool shows near his white moustache. He speaks with a touch of the Irish in his accent.

"Come in, come in! A bit late to show you the garden, but never mind. Come in and meet Peggy."

I stopped in the doorway, forgetting for a moment, Peggy?

The far wall was studded with the mounted heads of wild animals: spectacularly antlered sambur and spotted deer; a sloth bear, the fiercest beast of the forest; a pair of leopard; the monstrous tusked head of a wild boar. Below them, a rack of guns. By the door, a container held a miscellany of fishing rods and over-sized umbrellas.

"Good evening," A husky, slightly reproachful voice says.

A tall figure rises regally from a chintz-covered settee by the fire, holding out a limp hand to me.

"Oh! Sorry," I say like a schoolgirl.

"We were expecting you at four," she said. "We keep rather punctual hours here. Never mind. Come, let me show you your room."

We followed the flowing, pink silk robe down a corridor lined with hunting prints and waited while she opened a door. The room smelled of English flowers. Delphiniums, roses, sweet peas. And the soft scent of pinewood smoking in the fire.

A pink room, the colour of faded roses: the double bed with pink frilly pillows and a pink eider-down; pink camellias drifting over pale window curtains; pink silk-shaded lamps.

"Join us for a drink when you're ready," Peggy was saying. Suddenly she smiled, kindly, as if she had decided she liked us.

"Ring if there's anything you want." In the doorway she turned, her hand on the doorknob. "We dress for dinner, of course. Black tie. Dinner's after the Queen." and with that she drifted out. I wondered why I had the feeling that the room had not been used for a long time.

"What did she mean, 'Dinner after the Queen'?" I asked.

"After the nine o'clock news on the BBC."

❧

In the sitting room Douglas was busy at a mahogany drinks cabinet. Peggy, draped once more along the settee, looked magnificent. Her white fringe and short fluffed-out hair looked startling against her black eyebrows and the high colour of her cheeks. She wore a flowing green chiffon dress, a rope of jade beads and long jade earrings. One manicured hand held a cigarette in a long jade cigarette holder.

She beckoned vaguely to me to sit by the fire. Alistair was being sorted out with three inches of Glen Fiddich, then Douglas settled at last with his own drink.

"So your father likes the bird I sent him, does he?"

"It's on top of a bookcase near his writing table. It must have been a magnificent bird, Sir." Alistair said.

Douglas looked pleased. "I shot it on the Hortons."

He had been dining with friends when he had heard it and rushed out with his gun. It produced, he said, the most diabolical cry he had ever heard. A high-pitched shriek rising higher and higher; then a strangled cry, ending in an uncanny gurgling. Like the one I had heard on that first camping trip with my father to the Veddas long ago.

Silhouetted against a moonlit sky it had opened its beak to scream again when he fired. There was too much rubbish written about the confounded bird, he said. It needed to be identified finally.

The bird he had shot was a Forest Eagle Owl. It was not the only claimant for the title of Devil Bird. Endless articles had continued to appear in the newspapers.

I mentioned this mildly to Douglas.

"Damn fools," he muttered. "A cry can have a dozen interpretations. I still believe in my Forest Eagle Owl." And he would say no more about it. Instead he talked quietly, his eyes focused on the fire, about other things.

Then his old, blue eyes lit as he spoke of his rides over the wild Horton's, which I, too, had known so well. He spoke of its twisted trees bearded with grey-green Spanish moss; Giant Ciycas ferns which may have existed in the time of the sabre-toothed tiger.

We shared, too, the sight of the great Bear Monkeys and we had both walked a path alongside a snarling male specimen with only a thin curtain of underbrush between us. I too, had ridden fast over the Plains with the cold wind scouring my face, and the vision, through mist, of sambur grazing.

I wondered what he dreamed about?

Dreams filled and unfulfilled? House parties, friends, Country Clubs? The rule of the High Range aristocracy who abided by their own laws and founded the greatest estates in the island? He was one of the last of them.

❧

He handed me a yellowing photograph of a tall, bearded man in a solar hat, a heavy jacket and trousers sheathed in leach-gaiters.

"My father. He lived in a log cabin with a mud floor and thatched roof."

What had he felt when he first saw his land - a mountainside of primeval forest full of wild elephants and unknown dangers, which he would have to clear for coffee?

Douglas refilled our glasses, and the talk turned to shooting, birds, and fishing. Peggy watched sleepily from her corner. In the distance a parrot called harshly with Peggy's lisp "Douglash."

Once she aroused herself to tell me that when she was last in London she had bought a hostess gown, and when she returned had it copied in six different colours. This, jade green, with jade jewellery and a long cigarette holder to match, was one of them.

"Copied in Colombo?"

"No, dear. I NEVER go to Colombo. A tailor from the village. He sat on a mat somewhere around here and copied it." Then she drowsed again.

In the big stone fireplace, a log cracked and fell throwing flashes of scarlet and yellow up the chimney. A new branch caught fire, and took quiet strength from the fallen log.

Peggy choked a little on a snore and sat up brightly. Douglas glanced at his hunter and said, "Good God! Five minutes to nine - The Queen!" and rushed to the quietly murmuring radio to turn it up as it burst through a few atmospherics, into the British National Anthem.

"The Queen, God bless her!" Douglas stood erect, his glass held high.

"The Queen!"

Then we trooped in to dinner.

Peggy and Douglas sat on either end of the fourteen-foot mahogany table with Alistair and I in the middle on either side. The finest china, monogrammed silver and heavy Waterford glass, were set as if for a great dinner party, and there were only the two of us as guests.

The splendid seven-course meal was served with panache. Peggy toyed with an egg in a silver eggcup. When at last she rose, I rose too, leaving the men to their Port and cigars.

That night I dreamed that flames roared through the brushwood and felled forests of trees that scattered the mountainside. Screaming elephants tore through the bush; birds fell like bright sparks from burning trees, and small creatures, hare, mongoose, mouse deer, fled past the dark, naked figures of running men, and snakes oozed out of the forest.

When I woke, it was still dark. In the fireplace a log fell and threw a shower of sparks. But for a long time I could not sleep.

∾

"Douglas," I had asked, earlier, "When you returned from school after your nine years in England there must have been enormous changes - the estate must have been at its best?"

He interrupted irritably. "Yes, roads, towns, cars. But when my father met us on board the ship he had changed. Said he was fine. Everything was fine, he kept saying."

But for four years, blight had slowly destroyed his plantation. And his father had grown old. Most of the other planters had already uprooted their coffee, and were planting cinchona, cardamoms. Already there was a glut of them on the market. Douglas uprooted the coffee. "Every bush of it, with unshed tears as we did it," he said.

He planted cinchona, "But how much cinchona could the world absorb?" He planted cardamoms with the same result. Then tea seedlings were available - and took three years or more to become productive. Lanka had lain for centuries unaware of the productivity of its highlands.

I wondered what genes went into the making of a pioneer. Some harshness of his own land perhaps that he must seek another? Some affinity with the oceans that he must sail the seas to explore, to discover?

He was bright, animated, and at ease that weekend.

Sitting on the terrace before the house, I watched Douglas and Alistair return from their round of the estate. There was no sign of a stick this time. He walked with the quick springy step of the planter. It was Alistair who was labouring a little up the last incline.

"Lovely morning, isn't it?" Douglas was rosy with pleasure. "Good chap, your husband. He's got some splendid ideas for the factory."

Peggy was not at breakfast.

After breakfast Douglas took me round the garden. Against the backdrop of the mountains it was spectacularly beautiful. Douglas was in a quiet mood. Occasionally he snipped off a dead flower, and once even handed me a sunset-flared rose and a spray of lavender. The more I saw of him, listened to him, the more respect and liking I had for him. Under his small frame there was a core of obstinacy, charm, weakness, strength.

Peggy was talking animatedly with Alistair when we returned to the house.

Leaving Douglas to pour out more drinks and tea-talk, I wandered again onto the terrace. Nearby a small waterfall bubbled and flowed into a rocky pool with tadpoles. Kites flew crying overhead, and I thought for a moment of Herondale, my father's estate, now sold to strangers, then back to the early planters.

Once a week they gathered at the clubs of Bogawantalawa, Darawela, the Agras: names of districts to which planters and their wives from miles away, gathered for tennis, badminton, snooker, and in the evening danced to the music of a croaky gramophone. When it was irregularly wound, someone would have to hasten to wind it and it would screech into operation again. Perhaps a dated waltz, when lonely men pressed close against the few women present, and forgot for a moment their loneliness. And the girl-wives in turn, or even the older ones, would float quietly on a silent partner's arm, lost too, in dreams.

Occasionally a husband might close in on a couple, or there would be words. But whatever happened the ranks closed immediately; the sacred area of The Club was kept private and if necessary just judgment would be given according to their codes, and quietly ostracized, or forgiven by the time the club next met.

When Independence came, in 1948, many left. Those that remained learned with the change and adapted. Yet Douglas remained solitary and staunch to his own ideas. He died, shortly before estates were taken over by Government.

MY FATHER KNEW NOT only the island's history but also its poetry. He brought the buried cities of Anuradhapura, Polonnaruwa, and Mihintale alive for me. We followed the pathway of the great reservoirs built eight centuries ago, and set up camp wherever a peaceful place, always near water, enchanted us. Sometimes we hugged the coral coastline; and at other times the Land Rover plunged through jungle country where we camped with his beloved Veddas, and where I, the first civilized woman they had known, had grown to love them too.

Back at Wycherley we would pore over a large map in the library and his knobby finger, injured in some long-ago accident, would find an area where the road petered out into nothingness, and there we would go. We searched for a place called Kuveni Gala. All we knew about it was its name and a vague reference to the West Coast near Puttalam. At every hamlet we passed my father asked if anyone had heard of it. "No." At a very small village where as usual everyone gathered to stare at the Land Rover an old man stepped forward and said, "Why not? It is in the jungle where no one goes now."

ॐ

The scrub jungle was heavy with great vines that cut across our path. Now and then we saw droppings of deer, the spoor of leopard. We even passed a cave in which an elephant had left an imprint. Further on was another, deeper cave, its dark mouth festooned with thorny creepers. Inside, we plunged ankle-deep into mephitic bat droppings and were drowned in the shrill click of a thousand voices. Above us, clawing the cave-top, we saw in the flare of our torches black, satanic faces with red, malevolent eyes, and needle-edged wings. Further on, within sound of the sea, we found cut stone pillars of infinite age lying crookedly.

Kuveni Gala, said the old man, was the site where Vijaya, Prince of the Lion race, sent into exile with his seven hundred followers, had met Kuveni, the Vedda princess and married her. It was here, he said nodding his white head with certainty, that the Sinhala nation had been founded.

We travelled north to Jaffna and its islands, found small villages cradled in turquoise lagoons, and to Mullaitivu: all places that one-day would be ravaged by war.

The brown shoebox bulged until I found another to fill with more notes about Sri Lanka's places, customs, legends, and history.

The filing drawer of my desk was heavy with folders.

I was well into my first novel when the trouble began. Stooping to open the heavy file drawer, I doubled in pain. When I lumbered in to my father's library I saw, for a moment, the same, almost helpless look of immediate knowledge of what was wrong that had crossed his face when my mother became ill in Glasgow. Now it was his daughter whom he felt helpless to treat though he had successfully treated many similar injuries, but in my case complicated by a previous motor accident.

Spinal surgery has advanced enormously since that day in 1948. Then it carried risks with no certainty of success. In 1951 Alistair, my father and I flew to England to see an orthopaedic surgeon. He told me quietly that there was a 65% chance of success; the choice was left to me.

"Meanwhile do the exercises we've recommended, live as normally as you can within the limits of pain, and if you change your mind, send me a cable."

"Live as normally as you can," he had said. "Let's go, then!" I said.

We hired a car and with Anne, who had just left school, set out for the pre-historic cave country of Spain and France. One day in the middle of our tour I cried out "Stop!" I could not go on. So there we sat in our hired car and looked at each other. The tiny mountain village we had driven through seemed to lack a single hostelry.

There were no visible buildings, no other cars on the road. Then Anne spotted a building, almost hidden by trees and off she ran to return with eyes sparkling. "It's a new hotel. It's wonderful! We're the first guests!"

Built in the style of a luxurious hacienda it was appointed in lavish Spanish style. We were welcomed to lovely rooms. Beautiful girls with combs in their hair, waiters in Spanish costumes looked after us. The pain did not magically vanish but the stop for a few days with rest helped me deal with it. In a cobbled courtyard we dined by moonlight; a small band played old Spanish songs and a man with a silver trumpet lifted it to the moon, letting the notes echo through the hills.

I returned to Ceylon, determined at least to finish my book between bouts of pain.

Again pain streaks down my leg, numbs my toes and foot. I lie flat on my bed, allergic to pain-killers; seemingly allergic to exercises. Traction is tried, abandoned. My father who had pioneered spinal surgery in the island, hovers growling.

But I was still more or less immobilized and deeply conscious of the effect this was having on everyone around me, especially Alistair. Time passed, punctuated by visits from excellent doctors who hesitated to express an opinion under the critical eye of their one-time lecturer. A Viennese 'specialist' arrived in the island, and I persuaded my father to let me see him. He tried manual manipulation and I went into a screaming spasm.

Meanwhile I was missing out on the breathless social life that was rocking Colombo. I seemed to be missing out on everything that made life good and making normal life difficult for those I cared most about: Alistair and my father.

For Alistair it was the worst time. At the vital onset of his career in Sri Lanka, he was grounded at Wycherley with a supine wife, a dying mother-in-law and a rather unusual father-in-law. I had to persuade him to accept invitations, go snipe shooting with his friends and lead as normal a life as possible.

Would it have been far better if Alistair and I had had a normal life in a small house together? At Wycherley my father called the shots. Rest, he said in that voice that brooked no argument, rest is what will help cure Christine. Rest with medical care at hand. I cannot remember him telling me that specific exercise could have strengthened my back, though I am sure he would have told that to his other patients.

But I was singularly lucky; whenever possible I used to limp across to my mother's room. One day Alistair brought me a Golden Spaniel puppy I named Buff. It was a brilliant thought on Alistair's part. Buff's coat shone gold, his eyes wise, and he immediately attached himself to me and took over the lonely moments. On bad days he'd quietly lay his head against my hand on the side of my bed and watch me, his eyes worried. On good days he'd leap onto the stool at the foot of my bed and sit there, the gold plume of his tail wagging encouragingly. If I walked a little, he was at my side, guiding, guarding, encouraging.

Time passed. I could, at intervals, even walk a little. Visit my mother in the nursing home. When I took Buff to see my mother, she uttered the only words throughout her illness, "How sweet!"

꩜

I lie back on my bed and count my options. Write at least in pencil. Somehow finish the book. There was a lot to learn and think about.

There was my father's library. In the most casual way, he monitored my reading. By my bed, and for years to come were two books he had given me: *The Golden Sayings of Epictetus*, another of Marcus Aurelius. For the rest: plays, short stories of the world, poetry, new novels and classics. He subscribed to a weekly magazine *John o' London*, which recommended the best books to read. He sent for them and there would be discussions about them. It must have been a difficult time for my father – to have both my mother and me ill – but having me captive to his erudite but lucid discussions on books, eased his pressure a little.

Meanwhile, holding my writing pad at an angle, or typing when I could, my book was written, slowly and a long time later, finished. I first gave it to a dear friend and adviser, the clergyman of the Scot's Kirk of which Alistair and I were members. He returned it smiling.

"What shall I call it?" I asked.

"The Bitter Berry," he said.

One morning as I sat on our balcony watching a small striped squirrel tightrope along the stem of a wild creeper, it was suddenly illuminated by a beam of morning sunlight. I am not sure what happened then, but I remember calling out to Alistair, "Please, could you send a cable to Mr. Wiles at London. I'd like to have that operation - as soon as it can be done." Without question he nodded.

My father was leaving for the jungles that afternoon. When I told him about the cable, blithely he said, "What's the cast iron hurry?"

Alistair phoned from his office. The answering cable from the doctor named the day. We phoned my father that evening at the rest-house at which he had stopped before disappearing into the jungles.

"I'm flying to London on Tuesday," I said. This was Saturday.

Three weeks later I was operated on in London. Four years had limped by.

❧

The day I had my operation Anne was presented at Court with Alistair escorting her. Soon after he had to return to Ceylon and Anne enrolled at the secretarial college.

The hospital had me up on a chair by my bed next morning. I am on my own now, with the vow not to make a fuss. The room is filled with red and white flowers, roses.

"We think red and white flowers in hospitals are unlucky," a very young nurse tells me. I think beauty cannot be unlucky.

❧

Back at home, at four in the morning I'd wake, see the lights of the nursing-home shine softly beyond my windows, and shoving on a dressing gown, tip-toe downstairs to my den. Once the micro-biologist Jinadasa's work room, it was now converted into my study.

Writing at my desk.

Here I could type for hours undisturbed and the books were published in Britain. *The Bitter Berry*, based on the Herondale story; *I am the Wings,* inspired by the Horton Plains; *The Mountain Road* from a bus journey with Alistair from Jammu in India, to Kashmir.

My first book was accepted and the publishers wanted first option on the next two. Writing had been a way of life, and also an escape from the reality of constant pain which I was in until I flew to London and on a cold wet day in June, the day of the coronation of Queen Elizabeth, had my spine operated on. When *The Bitter Berry* and my other books were accepted few, if any, novels had been published abroad by a Sri Lankan woman. The distance, roughly six thousand miles, distanced local writers from making easy contact with publishers and agents.

The book that had absorbed me was accepted and published, then there was the second and third to write. And so on.

By then, when it was almost too late, I realized that life was passing too quickly and knew that in our lives ahead there could be no more room nor time to spare for writing.

৯

The other day I came across a novel of mine, never offered for publication. I am amazed at how meticulously planned it was. It lay curiously vulnerable as if some momentous happening had stopped me typing the final clean copy.

Later at a writers' conference in England I had consented, without consulting my publishers or agent, to write a cookery book. Hot afternoon hours were spent working out recipes experimenting with food on the back veranda upstairs at Wycherley while creative thought drifted away. But trouble was not far away. My agents were justifiably hurt. I had broken the ethics of the publishing world. I wrote one more book for them, then realized I had lost rare friendships; I also knew too, that my island was too far away for me to find another agent.

By the time we left the island, I had regularly written for the press and radio; the line of a novel about the Tea plantations (a very different one from the 'Coffee' book), lay abandoned.

After my father's death Vera del Tufo handed me an envelope with notes he had dictated about his early childhood and life, "For Christine to do what she likes with it."

I thought about my father who had died gently. He seemed very close. "There's a time to stay, and a time to go," he said, systematically tearing up note-books, letters, files, his own prescriptions, often compounded of ancient ayurvedic herbs to his own prescription. "*Why?*" I asked.

"My dear child, there will constantly be new discoveries better than these to take their place." Sitting back in his chair, he silently indicated a chair and said, "Sit."

"I'm going blind," he said. "Advanced Glaucoma." There was nothing much they could do about it, then.

As I watched him continuing to destroy things that were part of his life - photographs, negatives, manuscripts — he said, "There comes a time in life, Bunting, when we must leave things in orderly fashion for those that follow."

Now in the den I wrote at feverish speed. Through his dictated script I seemed to hear his dry, flat voice, and tears blurred the words, until I took over and began to write the Tissahamy chapter and on to the end, typing at times with eyes closed, memory taking over.

Surgeon of the Wilderness written and published in Sri Lanka after the death of my father, appeared in print when Alistair and I had left the island; I began a new chapter of my life. Now away from the island, I was to become committed to painting instead of writing.

Slowly but clearly I had become aware of an almost dangerous obsession with writing. I was at a point when my characters defied their creator and became their own people. It was heady stuff, but instinctively I hesitated.

My characters are taking over, I wrote in my diary. *Everything has a new clarity. I am more acutely aware of minutiae. As I move through the chatter of a cocktail party, I see without wishing to, involuntary movements of hands, eyes, under-currents of different meaning. It gives me more sympathy, more understanding perhaps of people, but in a way it was easier before to be social.*

"Don't over do the writing," Alistair would say, kissing the top of my head before he went to office.

One morning I woke late to the discordant cackle of the telephone. An agitated voice was saying, "We're phoning from Bishop's College. Lady M., the Principal, the girls, we're all waiting for you, Mrs. Wilson."

Waiting for me? Why? What day was it? Where was my diary? I'd promised to say a few words to the pupils at the opening of a new wing at my old school, Bishop's College, at nine o'clock. Now!

I was greeted coldly, given a bouquet of flowers and led past long-forgotten corridors to face the girls.

As they stood before me, with bright, beautiful faces and onyx-dark hair combed into identical plaits above crisp white uniforms, I was aware that I knew little about this new generation at an important era of development in independent Lanka. What would they grow into? What would be their influence in the governance of this island?

Our last years in Sri Lanka were taut.

Alistair, now Chairman of the Colombo Commercial Company, with a politically tense staff of about two thousand, was carrying an enormous load with labour troubles, growing unrest in the country, a surge towards Communism. These were uneasy days, with deadly trouble ahead.

One day I was told the police were downstairs to see me. A stocky police-woman with her arms akimbo, accompanied by two uniformed police officers stood arrogantly under the Persian lamp in the hall.

"You are one Mrs. Wilson?"

I nodded. She waved a sheaf of papers at me. "We have the necessary papers to search the office upstairs." Too stunned to speak, I led them ahead upstairs to the library. One of the men shrugged towards a small room adjoining. Once known as the Camp room, full of camp equipment behind wall-to-wall cupboards, it was now Alistair's office. Thrusting open drawers the man scattered a pile of letters onto the desk, and leaning arrogantly back in the chair proceeded to read them.

"Those are my husband's private letters from his mother," – I exploded. He continued reading. The woman gestured imperiously to me. "Bedroom! Your bedroom!" and swaggered ahead to stand before my wall-to-wall cupboards. "Open this!" she commanded with a flick of her thumb.

I had nothing there she wanted.

Suspiciously glaring at the beds as if she was on the verge of tearing them apart, she stumped back to the others.

A mumble of words in Sinhala, then out and away they drove in their heavy vehicle. Other Heads of Departments had their apartments broken into, their mattresses torn apart and searched. An ex-policeman and an unsatisfactory ex-CCC employee had gone to the police with some false story or other. Nothing came of the witch-hunt except inconvenience.

Trouble was simmering everywhere since the Sinhala Only Bill had been passed in Parliament. Tamil was OUT; English was wheeling downwards; Sinhala Only was *In*, followed by the mass departure of the intelligentsia and people whose main language was English. To England, America, Canada, Australia they went taking their families with them, sad for this island they had loved and would continue to do as long as they existed. Their offspring, in time would embrace, and grace, their adoptive new lands, but every now and then in their lives, and in their children's, the echo of a lost island would exist.

❧

In the spring of the next year we flew round the world on a shoestring. First to Australia where friends had invited us to stay, then briefly to New Zealand, Fiji, Hawaii, San Francisco, Arizona and finally New York, where we saw five plays in four days, staying always at the cheapest hotel we could find, for Lanka had placed strict limits on money for foreign travel. The allowance was £25 for living expenses; our air travel was by courtesy of Alistair's Company. We learned how to live on a diet of coffee, doughnuts and hamburgers, and the whole experience was fun. Our crazy tour ended in Glasgow where mail awaited us. We read it over a late breakfast in the dining-room of our Club, and while changing upstairs, I told him quietly about the acceptance of my book *Mountain Road*.

≈

In Scotland we met again my old tutor and our friend, Edward Scouller. He hadn't changed much. His small, screwed-up face with the bright eyes, ruddy cheeks, and wide smile revealing tobacco-stained teeth had grown a little thinner. But it was good to hear his raunchy voice with the dry, brilliant humour punched out in his rasping Glasgow accent. It was good to talk with him, and as always to realize how much more I had to learn. One thing stayed clearly in my mind. "For God's sake, Christine," he said, "Why on earth did you get involved with a cookery book?" I too didn't know why.

Alistair's father had died, but we were close to my mother-in-law. I took a photograph of her one-day when we drove her into the countryside, and picked blackberries. Her hat is set firmly on her head; her face, smiling; her punnet of blackberries better filled than Alistair's and mine put together. It was the last time we would see her. Living alone in the large house that had been in the Wilson family, she would accept no house help. "It ends with you having to help the Help," she said dryly. Shortly after we left, suddenly attacked by pain at night, she called her doctor. She passed away shortly after his arrival. Somehow, she had crawled downstairs to let him in.

≈

At this time I realised that there was something missing in the chemistry between Alistair and myself. It happens. I could find a dozen reasons to blame in myself: my idiotic back, the compulsive writing. On his side, too much work as he rose higher in his work and spent an increasing amount of time on necessary outstation visits. There were few quiet evenings at home. Instead, a demanding number of social engagements at which he shone. At one hilarious Christmas party, a woman turned to me and said, "How on earth did you two get together? Alistair with his outrageous, marvellously told stories, and you sitting there with your quiet smile?"

The pace increases. As Jane, my ayah fastens my cocktail dress, I smile at her small screwed-up face in the mirror. "Another party, Jane."

"Missee no tired?"

"Missee must not be tired, Jane."

Alistair in his Red Sea Rig - a short white mess jacket and black tie - swims into mirror-vision. He says, "Alright?"

"You look great!"

Three cocktail parties and a dinner lie ahead. I pick up an ice blue stole.

I think of the coming weekend. A trip with new young friends we were initiating into our particular kind of jungle trips, into which I myself had been initiated by my father long ago. There was no real secret to it, except acceptance of all the jungle offered, without complaint, without fear, with a readiness to learn and love.

I lived for those sorties away from the different jungle beat of the cocktail parties, dinners, dances.

≈

As Alistair and I walk hand in hand after dinner in the garden at Wycherley, we would talk. Perhaps we should move into a house of our own? As Chairman of the Commercial Company we could move if we wished into Acland House, the historic house dating from early British times. But leave my father, suddenly grown old and frail alone in Wycherley? "It'll come out all right," Alistair said. "Don't worry."

The engineering company, established at the latter end of the nineteenth century was a living, pulsing being that absorbed Alistair. Manufacturing a complete range of machinery for the tea, rubber and coconut industries, it had branches which carried out repairs and maintenance all over the island. To keep up with modern trends he had started an Apprentice Training School where new batches and existing staff were trained and re-trained under a specialized Training-Engineer-Instructor. In six months they were sent upstairs for lectures; and at the end of the year were absorbed into the work force. It was the only training school of its kind in the island.

There was hardly a week when Alistair was not busy visiting tea plantations throughout the island.

I needed to keep busy. I joined the photographic society, the wildlife society, any society that would fill my time. I went, whenever I could, on jungle trips to the wild life sanctuaries; sometimes only with Alistair's trusted driver, John Sinho, in a door-less jeep with a metal bar to hang on to. We had a new cine camera with which I was working and I wanted to make a cine of the seasons in the sanctuary. There were the two disparate rainy seasons of the Sou' West and Nor-East rains. Then our Spring, where one could almost watch the brittle trees break into leaf, and joyousness about the animals. The drought, where the sun scorched the trees, and the cicadas rustled in brown grass. Then, almost overnight, with a chiaroscuro of fireworks the monsoon would come with claps of thunder, forked lightning. Dry riverbeds filled within minutes with the swollen waters of the rains coming down from the hills. Then suddenly a break, the rivers dried overnight and the drought came. The rains, the Spring, the drought.

1952-1972

Goodbye to Ceylon

Leaving the old, both worlds at once they view
That stand upon the threshold of the new.
- Edmund Waller -

"MAY I BORROW JOHN Sinho for the weekend, please? I ask Alistair.

He knew I was trying to build my cine of the Jungle year; in drought, in spring, in blistering heat, and monsoon rains. He knew the last trip had been disastrously spoiled by rain, and that I'd just had a letter that the weather now was perfect. I become defensive. "I'm taking the four young Medical students I told you about. I wish you'd come, too."

Alistair's life as chairman of the company needed concentrated effort. Politics were beginning to involve his workers and required careful handling; but in spite of it there was the never-ending round of entertaining and being entertained at cocktail parties, dinners, being one moment the level-headed executive, the next; the judge and jury of a complex labour problem, then again the charming guest at a party. Only occasionally he managed a weekend away for us together, or a snipe shoot with some of his shooting friends.

I had to be let free. A full-time writer now, commissioned to write, often getting up at four in the morning to do so, but at the same time trying to be a good chairman's wife, there for Alistair yet not always succeeding, for he was locked away in his own life, I had to get away.

"Oh God," I think, "What has happened to us?" I could, I suppose, abandon writing – but then what? When we walk after dinner in the Wycherley garden as we always did, there are great silences for us, and the sullen sky suggests no answers. The moon is clouded, the stars and planets have put out their light, shadows reach across the lawn, and even the birds in the aviary settle surly on their perches.

It is only in those gentle wildlife sanctuaries that I find release from tension, and Alistair must go on his shooting trips to escape the lunacy of too much pressure.

Over the whole island, now, lay a strange feeling of change charged with menace. Governments came and Governments went. Ever since the benign president D.S. Senanayake died on Galle Face Green while out riding, and named his son, Dudley, instead of S.W.R.D. Bandaranaike, as his successor as prime minister, tension had grown. Dudley himself had said, "This is not my scene; I am an agriculturist."

Then his government fell. With the new Bandaranaike government, and the Sinhala Only policy, an anger was unleashed among the Tamils of the North and would eventually blaze into terrorism: The LTTE. There followed a time of restrictions such as this happy island had never known. The workers at the Company began to assert themselves; a mysterious fire broke out, which Alistair had to deal with. Just for a moment, just for this weekend, I hoped we would find a glimpse of our lost Sri Lanka.

"Yes, go on your trip," my husband said, turning back to his crowded desk.

I was grateful, for I had a strange feeling that my best-loved of sanctuaries, 485 square miles of it dedicated to conservation, was set too close to the militant North for its own safety.

❧

Nihal, Muthiah- called Tarzan, Anton and Sabha arrived at Wycherley after dinner. Next morning before dawn we were dressed and ready for the long drive to Wilpattu, and clambered into the jeep.

❧

1:45am. Downstairs in the Wycherley hall the three young Medical students who had arrived last night and settled to sleep for a few hours rose quietly. Upstairs I was already dressed in slacks and a safari jacket, picked up my camera. 2:00am was the starting time. The jeep, ready, packed, stood under the portico, the driver, John Sinho, standing by.

I remembered previous trips where we could be busy all day, wake at two in the morning, and drive away in a jeep or Land Rover. At dawn when the sun flushed faintly pink we would watch for wood-smoke and stop by the hopper woman.

"Who's got the eggs?"

"Oh-oh! I forgot them -"

"What?"

"Of course she hasn't."

Lace crust crisps golden brown and lifts cleanly onto plastic plates. Twists of paper with salt and pepper, crumb-cutlets of mince, green chillies. Flasks of coffee. In the distance we see the jacaranda blue-mauve highlands. Beyond, the land drops deeply into jungle country. Life seems perfect.

❧

"Auntie," one of the boys at the back of the jeep leans forward to tell me, "If you don't mind, we'll be stopping for breakfast at Nihal's." Nihal breaks in apologetically, "Auntie, it's a very simple place."

"No electricity." comments Tarzan.

Seated in front I cannot see their faces, but I hear a choked laugh. The jeep turns unexpectedly down a by-road and stops at a long, low house blazing with light. A gracious, elderly couple greet us, palms together in the age-old way.

"Welcome to our house."

"My Mother, Father," Nihal said.

Inside lay a table that could hold twenty, laden with all the lavishness of a complete Sinhala breakfast. Hoppers, milk-rice, pittu, curries of prawns, chicken, beef, vegetables of many kinds, trays of assorted fruit. But more than that was the gentle courtesy with which these were offered.

"The gods take care of you," they said as they saw us off.

❧

Our National Parks are small, intimate, beautiful. Here there are no endless plains with mammoth gatherings of elephant, buffalo, hippo. But great trees of Mara, Palu - the fruit of which bears love, Tamarind, Satinwood, Ebony, have grown for centuries. At every turn there are vistas with pools starred with water-lilies. Sometimes we may see little: perhaps the sight of a single amber eye, an indolent leg hanging from a branch from where he, the leopard can see but we cannot.

But wait long enough hidden near Leopard Rock, or another of his favourite places, and almost certainly he will appear, sitting proud on his rock as deliberately unaware of us as royalty might be.

A voice rings in my head: "Tell them, my daughter, how we searched the ground for clues, bushes where a deer rubbed velvet from his antlers in the season. How I taught you to study creeper-twined bushes as you pass for the sight of an eye-picker snake, slender as the vine it climbs. Explore dank roots of trees for orange-spattered fungi, deadly toadstools. Learn from droppings and pug-marks what animal passed this way and when. Study trunks of trees for claw-marks, nests; broken branches, where elephants have fed and passed not knowing they are destroying their habitat. Endless small creatures scuttle in the undergrowth, hide beyond our vision. And if there is nothing else to study, concentrate on the birds. Finally, tell them how we travelled cut off from civilisation by rising rivers, our food finished except for a tin of sardines and a tin of biscuits, tea, sugar..."

Our canvas tents were soaked - but Punchi, the Vedda girl,- found in the drenched forest twigs that would take light from her strikalight and flint and made tea for all.

"And then, Auntie?" I hadn't realised that some of this I had thought aloud and that four people were leaning forward eagerly. I had been thinking of a trek with my father long ago into the heart of Vedda country, in search of Tissahamy. It was then I had changed from a timid girl into a young woman who dared to do.

Painted storks move through a villu, a pond, their beaks sieving mud for fish; there are black-headed Ibis, egrets. Pelicans move over the water like small craft. Later, at another tank, a large herd of spotted deer drink.

Wilpattu is alive with beasts. Elephants, a sounder of pig burrowing, sambur belling or rubbing the velvet off the new growth on their antlers, a proud flotilla of pelicans on a lake. Tracks in the sandy roadway of many animals. The jungle throbs with bird-song.

I show the boys claw-marks of a bear on an anthill. Perhaps we may see the shabby rear of a black bear furtively shambling along a track with short-sighted eyes which make him all the more defensive when attacked. Then, rising on his back legs he charges like some mythic creature, claws raking, slashing, and lopes off, grumbling a little for he only wants to be alone, and eat his honey-bees or ants in peace.

"Bear!" Anton whispers as a mangy rear disappears down a track. "It's so small."

"Poor bear," I say.

Further on, the vehicle stops silently. On the branch of a satinwood tree a leopard stares down at us and we freeze, prepared for a long wait if necessary. But a wind-change brings the scent of a nearby kill, and we realise the leopard is waiting to drag it up a tree. I think hard. He appears to have no intention of moving. Why should he? He looks well fed and sleek.

Alone I might have waited indefinitely, but we were far from camp and it was well past noon. The pleading eyes of my friends are on me as I say to John Sinho, "Let's go back to the bungalow and return in the afternoon." He gives a slight nod of approval. The boys sigh.

"Why, Auntie?" Nihal asked as we drove back.

"I thought it time our leopard earned a rest. Time for him to eat, too." But on the way back we stopped again. A leopard on a branch, three quarters hidden among the leaves; below a sounder of pig scrabbling at a mud hole. A perfect leap down and it was over.

Never in all my travels have I seen as many leopards as we saw on that trip.

That afternoon we found the leopard and his kill: a young spotted deer - up the branch of another tree. Later we saw more leopards, one marking its site as he moved, silken muscles rippling. And once, four on a single tree, for it was the mating season, and all the park was alive with fecundity.

My father had been one of those who had most strongly advocated allocating 'this little gem' to be set aside for a National Park, which before had been a favourite sportsmen's reserve.

Small, intimate, clothed with some of the most beautiful trees in the island. Mahogany, *Kumbuk*, with rose-pink leaves in season, Teak, *Palu* and a hundred others whose names I do not know, there was an elemental sense of the past, for the ancient city of Anuradhapura lay not far from here.

~

"Why do we have this special love of leopard?" Tarzan asked when we sat under moonlit trees and a star-lit sky before dinner, with our drinks.

We had talked of many things, interrupted now and then by the sound of elephant breaking trees near us, the startled cry of a deer, the night jar, a sounder of pig at our small villu.

I'd read that weight for weight the leopard was the strongest of all animals His ways, different. We watched them mark their territory along some quiet track, stopping to urinate along the way.

In Africa, where he hunts best over wide plains, he is the quickest killer of all the beasts. But in our cramped jungles, and smaller plains, our leopards have to be more subtle.

The Vedda said they'd watched a leopard lie motionless under a berry tree monkeys frequented, with only the white tip of his tail twitching. Gradually the *wandura* draw closer, fascinated. Then one by one they get bolder, the leader bravely touches that mesmerising tail-tip, and in a screaming, scattering second the attack is over.

"Have you ever watched a kill?"

"No," I said. But one day I would, in Africa, watch, mesmerized a cheetah kill. As I write, I see vividly as on the day it happened, a streak of gold and black across great plains, whip-cord muscles taut, the small head focussed – the final spurt; the attack at neck and shoulders while back feet slash at buttocks.

Writing this, years afterwards it occurs to me that one needs the eyes of a peacock and the patience of the leopard, to see leopard, for they like kings, are privy to their territory. Even in Africa it cannot be hurried, we the uninvited guests, who if rough or rude, may see little.

Next morning we saw a black and white hornbill apparently pasted against the bole of a tree.

Pellets of clay and mud sealed the opening of his nest. Inside, his mate, de-feathered to make a downy nest for her young, had laid and hatched her brood, and here, incarcerated, she waited while her mate flew regularly back and forth, bringing each time some tempting morsel to feed the scarlet, wide-open beaks thrust out for food. Now a juicy, wriggling worm, next a bud, then a caterpillar, then a berry spiked on a stick.

Was it instinct that made his choice of protein and vegetable?

Later when his nestlings were ready, he'd tap open the sealed cavity and continue to feed his troop until his featherless mate and young could feed themselves.

On our last day we drove through barren country to a rock waterhole. Perched on the heated rock well above the water, drummed into a coma by the heat, we had grown silent when Nihal pointed. Below, breaking slowly through heavy undergrowth, an old, old elephant slowly dragged herself forward and stood, head drooping. Her trunk extended again and again, but not far enough, to reach water.

"She is dying," Saba whispered; the others nodded. I do not know how long we watched as she tried again to reach down, almost slipping, then stood at last, her head sunk between her shoulders, her tattered ears too limp to drive away the flies that hovered around her head. A young bear came, drank noisily and departed; another elephant, spry and strong, drank, showered water over himself and went. The old elephant tried again, and yet again. She was blind. Instinct had brought her here.

"Shall we go?" I said rising.

Behind us the elephant turned and with sagging shoulders moved slowly back into the shadows of her jungle.

In 1938 the 480-mile park of Wilpattu was opened to the public. In 1985 the LTTE, after an attack on the sacred Sri Maha Bodhi Temple at Anuradhapura attacked Wilpattu, shot its twenty-three personnel and used the park as a get-away place. The park was permanently closed in 1989. The rape of Wilpattu for its rare wood, its animals, and the decimation of its bungalows, began. The Park was closed until 2003. Now few animals are left, and they are frightened. New bungalows have to be built; dams and water tanks restored, more trees planted. Though the park is now declared open, only time and care can restore them. Nihal spoke to me of this yesterday. "Auntie, it will take time. We camped there. It is still beautiful."

Rangers, guards, some basically furnished bungalows which a party of six or eight could book for up to five days. We brought

linen, pillows, food; the cook at each bungalow cooked it —
extremely well as a rule.

John Sinho, our driver, knew these jungles well, and needed
no tracker, but he discussed with them where the best sighting had
been during the week and merely mentioned (for to mention them
by name was an unlucky thing to do) the best paths to take for
viewing. I too had already discussed what animals we hoped to see.
At the villus in the Park, perhaps fed from an underground spring,
there was always something to see. A lazy crocodile sleeping with a
wide smile on the rim; and in the tank, a darter; white herons,
sometimes a pelican or two swimming proud as steamers through
the water-lilies.

We rose to the scream of the peacock and the call of the
jungle fowl at dawn, drank tea and condensed milk, hot and strong;
then off for whatever the park would let us see.

It was agreed between us, that the name L-e-o-p-a-r-d would
not be mentioned, for that would be an unlucky thing to do. The
lore of the jungle must be observed.

"So what are we to look for?"

"Hope for nothing keep your eyes skinned for anything."

"I can see a crow," Tarzan says in a disappointed voice.
Everyone shouts him down. "There are no crows here!" "Yes, there
are!"

Nihal looking through his binoculars says softly, "There's
a leopard under that tree."

Sunshine slants on its golden body. He is aware of us, but
takes no notice. His eyes are focussed on a deer and her fawn at the
waterhole. We sit frozen. The deer moves closer to us. The leopard
vanishes.

I have seen many scenes like this in Sri Lanka, without
witnessing a kill. Death brings a different set of emotions. In Africa
I forced myself to watch what I remember as the incredible grace
of the drama. The endless plains, the fawn and the gold streak
stretched to its utmost, yet the leopard always a little behind, letting
its quarry tire, until it is ready to make that slashing sideways cut

with his paw, then the 'go for the jugular' attack, and the battle is fairly quickly over. That done, and a quick meal finished, it carries its quarry sometimes heavier than itself to be hidden up a tree.

No matter with which group of disparate friends I went, our lonely forests enthralled me. Sometimes I went, the only woman with three or four eager young students (I much older than they); sometimes with more sophisticated groups who had not visited the sanctuaries. Here, we left at more 'sensible hours' closer to six, and reached the conventional destinations. Going on safari with people you do not know can be a dangerous business; some could end in neither speaking to the other by the end of a journey, some in the creation of lifelong friendships. Sometimes I went with my father and Alistair. It was a different kind of safari with my father, it was he who had fought most strongly to make a wild life sanctuary of Wilpattu, and it was that which he loved most dearly. Yala had been a Sportsman's shooting reserve and was only later made into a wild life sanctuary.

Alistair, 1960

John Sinho, drove me on my lone safaris. Quiet with a good sense of humour, always respectful and courteous, he seemed to enjoy these trips as much as I did. In the time of rain, in seconds the brittle land could become filled with miniature rivers. The beautiful tanks (artificial lakes) were blocked. At last we stopped while the leaves dripped water and the windscreen wipers worked furiously over the steamed glass. "I wonder what leopards do when it rains," I murmured. Silently John Sinho pointed to a bush not two feet from us. Under it sat a beautiful leopard.

It was the leopard that interested Alistair and I most. There was another day at Wilpattu, my favourite game park, we had been round and round the small perimeter of the park, seeing everything except what I most wanted to see. At last John Sinho drove down a seldom-used game track, and stopped abruptly. On a tree above us sat the most beautiful leopard I have ever seen, a female, the sun shone on her coat, and it was gold, her tail swung languidly. On a lower branch sat another leopard. A third leopard joined them, touched the first one with a friendly paw, and vanished. And yet another, came, paused and left.

But things were different. Alistair was tiring but I was still passionate about this island. I was restless, going more urgently into the Game parks for quiet thought. I awoke to the cry of the jungle cock; the shrill *va-kovaaa* of peacock; tirelessly watched deer grazing, leopard stalking, marking their territory. Dawns came, went, flaring sunsets, royal purple darkening against silhouetted trees. Birds homing, owls awakening, the sound of the marble-dropping nightjar. Then the final, deep *whooo!* of the large owls.

"COME, HELP US, HUDU Hura, we are much troubled."

My father sat on his well-worn camp chair quietly smoking his cigar. A little distance away Veddas with whom we had lived and walked for sixteen days through forest they alone knew, crouched over the fire started with strike-a-light, flint and tree-bark cotton. The fire-glow touches now a thin shoulder, now a shaggy head, now restless eyes, ever moving and alive to every jungle sound.

This small group of people, perhaps twenty of them, were the purest Veddas on the island. Unsullied by civilization they were survivors of one of the oldest races in the world.

They still lived in the era of the food gatherers; seeking their sustenance entirely from the forests: honey from sheer rock faces; small animals trapped in crude deadfalls, or with the help of their much loved dogs: fish shot with miniature bows and arrows in some jungle pool lashed to a froth with cactus milk which brought stunned fish to the surface.

One of the Veddas began to sing a melancholy song to his jungle gods, *Bilindi yakka, Kande yakka,* and other gods of the hills and rocks.

Heen Kaira, a gentle man with soft eyes, stirred, and collecting young leaves made a sleeping nest for himself in the grooved roots of a tree. One by one the others followed suit. A dry twig snapped on the fire. Sparks spurted from the heart of a flame and died.

In the forest, creatures stirred. The marble-dropping nightjar ceased its ping-pong clatter.

It was always like this with the Veddas my father had known and loved for years.

It was a long time before my father spoke.

"It's difficult to know what should be done about these people. Is it right to let them continue to live the life of their ancestors - isolated - a prey to every illness, yet true to their ancient culture. But this way, they will surely die as a people. Should they be brought closer to civilization to survive differently?

Their only contact with civilization was my father. He continued to visit them whenever possible, treat whatever illnesses they had. But it was not enough.

Back in Colombo his passionate letters to the newspapers brought letters, editorials, and finally a promise of government help.

In place of their mud-and-wattle thatched huts, simple houses with corrugated iron roofs were built for them nearer civilization. A people who had only known barter - a haunch of venison in exchange for an arrow head - learned to work for money: and to realize that their antiquity as a race had a commercial value. But that was still ahead.

The original Veddas of Bingoda did not like their neat houses. They continued to keep themselves apart from the encroaching villagers. Already their proximity had brought sadness. They still sang their ancient songs, danced their ritualistic dances, shook their shaggy locks wildly as their bare feet stamped the rhythm.

Gomba was one of my favourites. He was a strong young man who had married the most beautiful girl in the clan. Living close to a village now, he had walked there to buy some necessity, when a villager stopped him. Did he not know, he was asked, that his wife had been unfaithful to him?

Gomba rushed back to their small hut and hacked her to pieces.

My father received a pathetic letter dictated by the Veddas. "Our beloved and honoured *Hudu Hura* (White Brother) Much sadness has come to our clan… Only our *Hudu Hura* can help us…"

I never knew what my father wrote in reply. But at the court hearing the rural development officer pleaded for Gomba, and begged that the case be treated with compassion. The allegation about Gomba's wife was not even true. A villager was in fact to blame, said the Veddas. Gomba was sent briefly to the mental hospital for treatment.

≈

The twenty-five years of Alistair's work in Lanka were studded with many visits with my father to the jungles. Sometimes we re-visited his favourite people at Bingoda; at other times we went to Dambana in the south of Ceylon where the Vedda settlement, closer to encroaching villagers was slowly being assimilated by a different culture. Here, the tendency to become show people for tourists was saddening and inevitable. Their forests had gone, or rather, what was left to them could not provide adequate hunting grounds - even if hunting was permissible, which it was not. The private dignity of people was eroded by the laughs and sniggers of tourists. The bows and arrows rotted away and new ones replaced them. They sang their tribal songs for curious crowds.

≈

Around us the political situation changed, and changed again.

D.S. Senanayake was succeeded by his son Dudley Senanayake, and he in turn was followed by S.W.R.D. Bandaranaike who, rejecting his predecessors' concept of plurality introduced the Sinhala Only formula, and from then on life in Sri Lanka became different.

Alistair was only fifty-five when he retired from the Colombo Commercial Company. The mandatory age for ex-patriots.

He was slim with the tennis he played, our early morning swims, his eyes bright with the challenge of running the vast company.

He reminded me flatly one day, "I retire at the end of this month, you know."

I swung my typing chair round and stared at him. The familiar vulnerable look had been replaced by colder eyes, a stronger mouth; there was a harder ring to his soft, Scottish voice. Agate eyes met mine. The months had slipped past swiftly.

"You mean it! Oh my God, so soon! Can't you stay on?" He stared at me.

"Well, I mean, is…" I floundered. "Then? What?"

"It's been a lonely business being the only European left in a firm of two thousand people," he said coldly. "I've tried to tell you…"

"Let's sit down. Talk it over."

"There's nothing to talk over. Ceylonisation of the company, and I, the only European left in it," he began and shrugged. "It's time for the others to take over, to know when the time is right to go."

There was nothing to say. I knew he was a well-respected and much-liked chairman. I knew how, at the beginning of his ten years as chairman, the British staff had been slowly, inexorably, whittled away until he was the last of them left in this British-owned Company. Occasionally he'd say wryly, "It's cold at the top," and leave it at that, for he was a typical Scot whose emotions lay deep. He had told me about it lightly, but I, engrossed with writing, and the publication in England and Germany of my first two books, with a third on the way, had not really absorbed his depth of feeling.

We talked for a long time, and I wanted to take my wounded husband in my arms like a child, comfort him, and perhaps cry a little with him. But, strangely, we had grown out of the old, sweet habit of doing so, though we still walked hand in hand in the jasmine and frangipani-flowered garden.

৵

Alistair came into the library at the end of an endless day and looked at me strangely.

"My resignation has been accepted," he said for the second time. "With regret. We go."

అ

The Nursing Home would continue to be run by others, as it had since my father's retirement. Wycherley would remain more or less as it was as I desperately pleaded, with Jane, my faithful maid and housekeeper for twenty-five years, and old Raman, the cook to look after my dog, Spot, and the house. Crazy. But that's all there was time for. At his last big farewell party for his staff, people were already beginning to circle round the next possible chairman. We would leave as soon as possible, he said again, immediately after it, and when he used that tone of voice there was no equivocation possible. Books? They were sorted out as best we could. I had intended leaving them one day to the Archives or a university library, but there was no time for that now. Many things were abandoned; lost in the mad rush to give away whole wardrobes of clothes, empty drawers. From a desk drawer of my father's a gold pen given by a grateful patient had disappeared. In another drawer that had held a treasured personal letter from Dickens to my grandfather van Dort, who had known him in London in the days of sailing ships, along with his book of stamps, had vanished.

At the bottom of a wardrobe of my mother's I found a tiny packet with a yellowed tissue paper cover: inside, a soft, light-brown curl. In minute letters in my mother's handwriting was written: "Yvonne's hair." Her lost baby.

అ

Strangely, there had been a coolness between my father and I in the last few years. He hated the tip-tap of my shoes along the polished corridor between our rooms and would shout, "Those bloody high-heeled shoes of yours; what rest can I have?" So I'd walk barefoot with them in my hands. I'd order some special meal for his lunch or supper, and ask, "Did you enjoy it?" and he'd reply grumpily, "Not much." I'd sit on the side of his bed, look at the great veins that snaked under the frail tissue of his skin and wonder if one day my hands, too, would become like that. A great sadness filled me for the father I had known.

To Alistair, who often carried him, fragile as a bird into his library to stare blindly into space while we tried talking to him, he answered monosyllabically. Maybe we'd tried too hard, maybe it showed; he sat grimly silent, hurting physically. Only Anne could work magic with him. She could make him laugh at her outrageous stories.

In the hot afternoons she would dash upstairs, stroll into his bedroom where he lay trying to rest but could not, curl up on the settee against the wall by his bed, and chatter away. What did they talk about, I'd ask after seeing these miracle changes in him. "Anything and everything," she'd answer, "his philosophy, mine, the world as he saw it, about you, Mummy."

"What about me?"

L- R: Alistair, Liz Banks, Henning, Anne, Daddy, Me,
Richard Piman, March 1959

"Your shoes tapping the floor!" Her smile vanished. "Seriously, Mum, he worries very much about you. We all do. You've grown away from us."

"Rubbish!" I flashed back, really hurting, "What am I supposed to do?"

"Don't worry, Mummy. He quoted something to me - I've forgotten bits. 'For each man kills the thing he loves; some do it with a sword, and others with a word.'" I then remembered that he used to recite that same verse to me too, long ago in connection with my mother.

Anne put her arm over my shoulder. There were times when this daughter of mine could be as adult, as strengthening as anyone I knew.

We, Alistair and I stood by, did not intrude in the shared laughter when my father would say something particularly outrageous and Anne would ruffle his cobweb frail hair, and tease him, making that grim taut face relax a little. Sometimes she would come with her husband, Henning, and Pia-Christina, their beautiful flaxen-haired daughter. She and Pia-Christina were the joy of his heart. He saw too much of us, perhaps... or not enough?

Then Anne, Henning and Pia-Christina were off on leave to Denmark. Days passed.

❧

A journalist comes to interview me. I tell her, "Please excuse me if we make this very short. My father is very ill upstairs."

I go through the half swing-doors of his bedroom to say good night. He is a very old and tired eighty six.

"Goodnight, Daddy darling," I say in the same old way I've always said.

"Night, Bunting."

"Would you mind ringing that bell," he says.

The bell to the Nursing Home.

"No," I say quietly. "Please."

His voice gets strong suddenly, "Damn-it, Bunting, I want Vera for that injection!"

"No," I say and shake my head at the grey-haired man who had once been the chief attendant in his wards at the General Hospital.

"What am I to do, Missee? He is our Master," he whispers as I leave the room.

᠀

Shortly before Anne, Henning and Pia Christina were due to return to Sri Lanka, he passed away with the sound of the jungle cock that lived in his aviary in his ears.

They said nearly a thousand people came on that day in September. But I stood alone at his graveside unaware of anyone, not understanding why Anne had not come in time. Then later, they too, left — to settle in Demark permanently. Suddenly everything was crumbling around me.

There were two books I had wanted to write. I packed my notes on them into two cardboard boxes and knew I would never write them now.

"I MUST GO AND say good-bye to the Veddas," I said.

Alistair looked up from his packing, and shook his head. We were leaving Sri Lanka next week. Whether for a few months or forever I did not know; I was in no state to know.

"Sweetie, be sensible! You'll never get through to them in this weather," my husband said.

"I can leave in the Land Rover tomorrow, leave before dawn and return the same day."

Outside, the monsoon thundered as I crept away to phone the Meteorological office again. "What's the weather like? Can I get through to Maha Oya? I've got to say goodbye to my father's Veddas. We're leaving Lanka."

The man knew about my father and the Veddas who had called him their father. The monsoon was at its height, he said.

"I'm going," I said. I had already sent a telegram to Maha Oya to expect me.

"Good luck, then," he said, and "God take care of you."

The Land Rover smelled of Rexene, damp leather and other jungle trips. John Sinho who had driven us through many miles, drove silently, fighting skids and rock falls as we went northwards. The windscreen wipers drove back and forth against misted glass, lit now and then by lightning, followed by the crash of thunder.

"Not very good, John Sinho. Do you think we'll be able to cross the river?"

"Can't say, Missee, *Deviangé pihiteng*." God willing.

They lived beyond three rivers when I first met them. I remember when, with my father, I trekked there, my young, unused muscles hurting with the pace on hot, baked earth, feet in canvas boots blistered. Remembered following the frail figure of my father, and ahead of him the lithe, swinging body of Tikkiri, the son of Tissahamy, the murderer whom in the end I never met!

And that poem my father wrote,

> *"Do you remember us when we are gone,*
> *you solitudes,*
> *as we do you,*
> *like friends upon a sojourning?"*

Today, unable to reach us they would be squatting in their mud and wattle huts, gazing at the rising river, as we had watched it together when they and I were young.

I remembered the heavy drip of rain on canvas. My father placed a twig halfway between the tent and the river. We sat crouched, ten, twelve of us pressed close in the foetid tent. The mud-brown torrent rose, twigs, branches, uprooted shrubs hurtled down the river. The mocha-cream foam at the edge of the water reached the implanted twig. "Time to move on," my father said.

I open my eyes. We have stopped before the small house of the district officer, who comes towards me bearing an umbrella. "So, you came," he said, beaming, "They are there." He points towards the river.

They stand in a huddle on the far bank of the wide river. Men, women, children, standing in the fury of the monsoon, greeting us with a cry that the wind carried away. But I feel the tears in their eyes that the rain washes away, and hear their grief, which is mine, too, held in an endless moment.

Five of the strongest men swam across the river to meet me, and putting their hands on my shoulders in the Vedda greeting wept with me for the loss of the man they had called Hudu Hura.

But I could not let them stand there; so I went back to the house, drank tea that did not warm or console, and asked how things had been for the Veddas.

Another two, from a clan of only thirteen, had died, one a baby at childbirth. As civilization edged the forest back, until there were no forests, there would be integration with the village cultivators, and this race of a thousand years or more, would be only a story told.

As I stood in the bedroom I felt someone behind me. It was Gomba.

"Ah, Gomba!" I said, "it is good to see you. I must photograph you." We went outside where two others waited. "Please stand together," I said. As they stood together, arms over Gomba's shoulders, I remembered one of them was Gomba's father-in-law, the other, his dead wife's brother. Where else in today's society I wondered could this have happened.

$$\boxed{1973\text{-}1993}$$

Africa, Africa

Africa was full of strange things
- Phillip Pullman -

I REMEMBER LITTLE OF our going, or who, if anyone, saw us off at the airport. I think we went alone. Hand in hand, close yet distant. Emotionless, I saw shapes pass and did not know what they were; went mutely on board our flight to London and cannot remember anything of the journey.

In London we stayed with friends until we found accommodation.

The last flat on the Richmond House Agent's list was in a large apartment block, its door open. Inside a young woman in jeans sat on the carpet playing with her baby.

She gestured towards the rooms. "Please look round."

When we returned she rose, just a slip of a thing, too thin, not more than nineteen, her baby held close, her face suddenly tense.

"You'll take it?"

We glanced at each other uncertainly, and nodded.

"Look! Take it," she said tensely. "I'll throw in the carpet for the price."

I sat alone in the house of our friends. They had gone on holiday. Alistair had flown off on an unexpected consultancy in Rwanda. It was a lovely old house, with the smell of dusty books, walls hung with gilt-framed portraits of famous ancestors and stairs that creaked. The wind whistled down fireplaces that were not lit until a particular day in September.

Crouched over a small two-barred electric heater I watched rain lash against the windows and fall in steady rivulets. Wind stripped the trees and plastered the English lawn with autumn reds and yellows.

I missed my parents, Sri Lanka, Wycherley, with all my being.

The rain had stopped when I woke at midnight my face wet with tears. I had been, in my dream, in a cathedral of endless corridors, leading nowhere.

A few nights later I woke abruptly. Somewhere downstairs the telephone was ringing insistently. It was still ringing when, with my dressing gown scabbed over my shoulders, I ran downstairs to answer it.

"Mrs. Wilson?" The voice was harsh.

"Yes. Who is it?"

"If you think you're going to have that flat with the carpet thrown in, you're mistaken. Alone, aren't you? Tell him that. We're serious. If he doesn't pay up we'll bloody well break in." The phone went dead.

Alistair, when he returned and we moved in, fitted double locks on the doors, had a peephole inserted but every time there was a ring at the door or the telephone went, I started. Sometimes I'd wake from a nightmare and wandering over to the windows six floors up, look across at the road where buses moved beneath hazy lamps, and dark-coated figures hurried, faces hidden in upturned collars. Out there, someone waited.

But no one believed me. "She's over-reacting with the change," they said.

Alistair, was out when the second call came. "If you think you're going to get away with moving in without paying for the carpet you're wrong. I and my friends will break in, do you hear?"

I rang Alistair at his office. This time he and our friends took it seriously. On investigation they learned that the girl and her baby had vanished. She had never been married to the father of the child. He had just been released from prison.

With the help of a lawyer an injunction was put on the man. The security people of the apartment block were alerted. But it had only needed that to send my mind skittering. Suddenly I cracked.

The expensive clinic was good, though I have little idea of what the treatment was, nor cared. It wiped my mind clean of memories. A peaceful feeling. Most of whatever time was my own I spent in the art section and painted abstracts in strong colours that gradually toned down to pastel. And in a pastel mood I returned with a calm in which Alistair did not completely believe.

On that Saturday afternoon when the telephone rang I was sewing placidly, and did not even look up.

There was tension in Alistair's voice as he answered with a clipped "Yes!" then drew a block towards him and began to write rapidly. Outside traffic hummed, but in this room there was only the scratch of his pencil, the rustle of paper as turning the foolscap page he continued to write. I put a tentative hand on his shoulder, but without looking up, he slightly shook his head and continued writing. Then slapping down his pencil he jerked his head at me and asked, "How would you like to live in Kenya? Yes or No? Quick!"

"Oh yes!" I said.

❧

We had visited East Africa twice in the sixties when white policemen still directed traffic and white assistants stood behind the counters of many shops. The Mau Mau had left the country bruised, and we were warned to be careful.

With strictly limited currency we had little money to spare for tourist safaris, so, chancing our luck, with only our knowledge of Ceylon's jungles, and a map of Kenya, we optimistically hired a Volkswagen and drove joyously together into the wild lands, the Serengeti and the Ngorongoro crater.

Alone, we drove, ant-beings, silent, across the mighty Serengeti. It was good to be young, to take risks and find them worthwhile. And now, thirteen years later, to still feel that core of excitement re-kindle at the thought of returning to Africa.

We spent the first night in a tented camp, with a thatched toilet some distance away. The next morning it was ringed by the pug-marks of a large lion. It was our first reminder that we were in lion country.

It was mad, it was fun, and sometimes we were scared to death.

IN OUR CORNER OF Africa there was no room, no time for memories we had left in Lanka. This was virgin territory in which, dear God, we could make our own small histories, contribute afresh, and begin again.

There would be no more writing to devour us both.

This was an unspoken thing between us. During our time in Sri Lanka I had begun writing seriously about a Lanka I cared about. The articles were written fast, sometimes with tears blurring my eyes; sometimes at four or five in the morning, when driven by compulsion, I'd creep downstairs at Wycherley to my den, and set words clattering. From this, emerged the first novel. But it was a strain. My writing was becoming an obsession.

❧

In Africa I felt as if all the old, raw places inside me had been swept away, and it was good. In Sri Lanka, all the time, there had been the fret in the background, and often very much in the foreground, over the ever-shifting balance of different governments, different kinds of stress.

I had fought, with my father, for declining forests, for elephants cut from their feeding grounds and water; for downcast people, and left knowing there is a time and a place for everything, and my time, my place would be filled by others.

And so I let go instead, open to new experiences, new spells, new smells, a new beginning. Abruptly, we were both truly happy. For the first time there was no need to rush anything. We could take things slowly, in whatever sequence we liked.

❧

We came to Africa like children to a new school armed only with essentials purchased for a two-year stint in Kenya, and several cases of books.

Under the benign umbrella of the World Bank, I, for the first time in my life, identified with a community.

At the Welcome to New Comers' party intelligent, smart young wives of many nationalities gathered. Have you found a house? Where? Good, join the New Muthaiga crowd. It isn't finished yet; we need to furnish it. Don't worry. Call us for any help you need. I'd never known anything like this.

"There's a lecture by Mary Leakey on Tuesday. You should join the Know Kenya Course."

"Gillian's doing a super course in tailoring and dressmaking. Michelle and Joanne are doing Cordon Bleu. There's an excellent English teacher of painting."

"There's literally nothing you can't learn here if you want to," said Joyce Craike, the doyenne of the World Bank.

I wanted to join them all, and for us, above all, there were the vast plains and the National Parks. But a house had to be found. Alistair was now travelling extensively in East Africa on World Bank missions, and I had time for anything I chose to do.

❧

We found our perfect house on a newly-opened site on a hillside 6,000 feet above sea level. Flanked by a vast forest reserve and not quite finished, it lay surrounded by a clutter of builders' materials. Mountain light poured through its steel-framed windows, sliding glass doors led to a covered terrace that faced the forest.

Off the hall an unfinished stairway led to an unexpected lower floor scooped from the hillside. Capacious, airy, its fireplace matching the fireplace in the sitting room above, it led through sliding glass doors to its own smaller terrace at ground level. Beyond, over an acre of slithery red mud, half a dozen Kikuyu women bent like hairpins, planted grass.

Me in Kenya

George, the first of our staff, appeared one day when we were visiting the house. He sauntered towards us with the grace of an animal, arms swinging, a pink silk shirt with a button missing sloping carelessly off one shoulder. "I am gardener," he said in his soft African voice. As we walked round our barren land, part rich with forest loam; part scoured deeply where the dig had been too great, he walked ahead assessing its slopes and valleys. Some instinct told me he had studied it before, for George had a special gift for creating gardens from nothing, and whatever God he believed in had surely sent him to us.

He had worked at one of the best plant nurseries in Nairobi.

"I like to be your gardener," he said, hitching up his shirt a little. "Start tomorrow."

From time to time, as we waited in our cottage at the Norfolk for the house to be finished, he visited us. He needed plants, he said, bulbs, sapling trees, flower and vegetable seeds. He would select them. Enthusiastically we drove to the great plant nurseries, walked through aisles of bougainvillea, flowering trees, roses, and flowering shrubs, and he selected what he wanted. He chose flowers and creepers of strong colours to offset the stone facade of the house; multi-coloured bougainvillea to cascade down the long bank flanking the forest; misty blue Jacaranda to give depth to the further end of the garden, and for me a wild cherry tree near the high terrace where I could always see it, and a bird-bath near it so that the myriad birds of the forest could visit.

Alone in his plot he created his garden as an artist paints with colour. As he worked he sang with a soft sweet voice, always the same haunting tune. One day I asked him, "What is your song about, George?"

"A man was going up a hill in a little car," he said and trilled a fragment of his song, which seemed to go, "Tra-la-la-la-laa…"

"Then he met a young girl as he went –" and another bit of crooning.

"Then the car stopped and he said he could not mend it," George said; and throwing back his head with the peppercorn curls, he laughed a deep-throated laugh full of youth and freedom.

From him, too, I learned my first Swahili words: *Pole Pole* said with a long "e". According to how it was spoken, I learned that it could mean many things, compassion in times of trouble, as a warning for motorists, but the one I liked best was "Slowly, slowly." It was a good word to know, for everything moved forever to a time clock of its own in this strange and lovely country.

We woke early that first day in our new house at Spring Valley. It lay about 6,000 ft above sea level, the sky the deepest blue I had ever seen, the air, sharp and cold with a touch of frost challenging us to throw back eiderdowns, fling open windows onto a new garden with the smell of raw earth and young grass; plants and trees breaking into leaf, their smells mixed with the essence of the Great Karura forest which edged the length of 'our' property.

We looked at each other. "Unbelievable, isn't it?"

We were here for a two-year stint with an option of extension. It was impossible to think beyond the present: this was now. Beyond, stretched all Africa. Our previous two glimpses of it had been experienced as amateur tourists on our own, in a small hired car and a meagre travel allowance from Sri Lanka. This time we were here to live.

We unlocked the iron grill that sealed us in a safety wing in case of a break-in and walked through the house onto the balcony beyond which George had planted the small cherry tree, and beyond again, the depthless greens of the forbidden forest. In another forest link in the drought, thousands of thirst-driven beasts thundered mindlessly to Tanzania in their search for water. Would we be lucky enough to see it?

అ

We were still at the Norfolk when one Saturday afternoon a man loped towards us across the garden, in a loudly checked tweed jacket, a hand in his pocket and a jaunty cap on his head. As he approached he removed it, and casually asked, "Wanting Cook-Houseman?"

His certificates were glowing. Only he seemed not to have stayed long anywhere.

"Why?" we asked.

He shrugged. "When it is enough, it is enough." He, unlike George, spoke excellent English. "I make bread," he said expertly changing the subject. "Good bread. Cooking, washing, ironing. Anything."

"Wash cars?"

His whiskered face broke into a wide smile. "I like cars too-too much!"

"Your name is written here as John Wachira. What do you prefer to be called?"

He said with dignity: "Wachira, of course." Then shrugging again, "Not important. Wachira or John. I do same work."

"Wachira, of course," we said.

"I think I like to work with you," he said.

What appealed to us particularly was that he was mentioned as a good camp cook and safari man. The rest would follow. Maybe he'd even get me over the birth pangs of becoming a Kenya housewife, which was to be different from anything I had known.

འ

We bought furniture, some in shops, some through newspaper advertisements. One British woman, selling up after forty-five years in Kenya was sad. "Kenya's changed of course, after independence," she said, "It was wonderful before."

"We think it's wonderful now."

"You're new. You'll change your mind." With a shrug and in a changed tone, she asked briskly, "D'you want a gun?" and drew from an inner, steel-lined, hidden cupboard, a rifle.

"I don't think so." The .22 my father had given me, and Alistair's rifle we had placed in Police custody. The Mau Mau trouble was well over.

"You may," she said obscurely. "We did, during the change."

Nevertheless, back at the house, iron grills were fitted against the glass double doors off the terrace; another shuttered the sleeping area from the main body of the house. It was the policy of the bank to safeguard its people. We had two security guards, a day and a night one. Above the beds a bell push security system connected with a nearby security office. If pressed, yet another signal, a klaxon, would shriek across the hills and valleys.

Only one thing worried me a little. We had no telephone. It took time, they said.

Alistair's work entailed visits across East Africa. It was a lonely feeling, when he was away, like the time at Herondale, when I listened to the wind howl and the storm beat the tea bushes; only here there was a cosmic awareness. Above the dry whisper of the trees in the vast forest adjoining us, creatures I'd never seen were stirring. All Africa stretched before me.

Sirens shrieked, it seemed from our own quarters, and went on howling, echoing, re-echoing. The huge Alsatians in the house opposite were barking like crazy, ours pitched in, and down the road, all the other dogs were barking, too.

"That's from the house opposite, Loraine's." Alistair said, shoving on his dressing gown. I followed suit and we hurried across from our garden to the big white house across the way where our neighbour lived alone. Our guards Stephen and Mbuti were already there. Lights blazed, our neighbour, in a dressing gown and curlers stood calm, her face pale, not with fear but anger. "They disappeared over the wall back into the forest as soon as the security men saw them," she said. "Did they take anything?" "No, I don't think so." The Alsatians still barked gratuitously. "Coffee?" she offered automatically. "Let's have some coffee." There was nothing much we could do afterwards, except to offer help at any time, and leave.

I found I was trembling. With cold? It was hitting 17 degrees, and my teeth were chattering. My slippered feet slithered in a cold, wet rut, and Alistair grabbed my arm.

"Suppose it's us next time." I said.

"Most unlikely," he replied. "They seldom go for the same area."

We sat cupping our hands round mugs of hot chocolate in our sitting room, I, with my feet curled under me on the blue settee. Hoping the cocoa would prevail over black coffee.

"Anyway," Alistair said, "It'll be nice to get away this weekend." It was a long weekend, our first, and we had planned to visit the South Coast in the new car which had just arrived from England.

๛

Before the time of the Great Rains, immense clouds gathered, built into giant thunderheads, and massed again in gargantuan shapes. "See, Alistair! A dragon, unmistakably a dragon. No! It's changing! It's a Titan now…!"

They built up, great feather pillows, tossed eiderdowns, restless, wind-blown, forming, reforming one on top of the other, and then drawing apart. I would stare in wonder each evening as we drove back after collecting mail from our disreputable little post office.

"Come, let's drive on and discover what's on the other side of the hill," we'd say together, for once again we thought alike.

Then we'd drive slowly past the eucalyptus-scented hillside and on, where there were no trees, no buildings. Then abruptly following random trails, we'd find new places with a curling stream or a deep green reservoir edged with arums; a small church, or women and boys selling plums, apples, bananas, fresh melons. We loved those gentle evenings, which we could repeat a hundred times, yet always find something new.

Back at the house, with its deceptive cottage façade, and its secret lower floor that walked us straight into the garden, we'd sit on the higher terrace (the cherry almost ready to bloom), and look at the forest, wondering what beasts wandered there. It was time then, for drinks and smoke wreathing up from Alistair's pipe, his hand reaching for mine.

➴

All round us new shops were springing up. At Westlands, our neighbouring shopping centre, a well-stocked book shop opened, stacked almost beyond reach of tall ladders; designer clothes shops; better butcher's shops; vegetable *dukas* piled high with fresh strawberries, peaches, mushrooms, well-displayed vegetables. But still we stuck with our Spring Valley *dukas*. In the time ahead when there were power-cuts, five times the main *duka* was broken into and we would find Mr. Lalvani, his plump and efficient wife and daughter in melancholy gloom with hurricane butties, (as few as possible, just enough to see), and he, still uneasily sitting on his too-small stool, squirrel-eyes narrowed to pin points as they followed the course of every customer.

"I am so sorry, Mr. Lalvani. Have you reported this?"

"What good reporting!"

❧

A few minutes drive from our house, and opposite the bubbly stream that gave the valley its name, the small shopping centre carved from the hillside supplied most of our daily requirements.

One-eyed Amos the flower-seller was one of the first friends I made there.

As I drove up for the first time, a covey of boys seated on the veranda floor with buckets of fresh flowers rushed forward pushing roses, carnations, gladioli from the most glorious array of flowers I had ever seen. "Roses, Mama, champagne roses, carnations, what you like, very cheap."

Among them, quiet, was one-eyed Amos, an old felt hat half over his blind eye, a tired bunch of champagne roses in his hand.

"Jambo, Mama," he said quietly.

I bought his flowers, and afterwards it was always from him I bought flowers. Sometimes they were splendid and his face was wreathed with smiles, though his stock was smaller than that of the others, sometimes very meagre, and weary as himself. But there was still the gentle "Jambo, Mama," the smile of understanding and mutual respect that lay unspoken between us.

Days, weeks passed, a year or more, and it was the same. It was only Amos's flowers I would buy to welcome friends back from leave, to celebrate a birthday, a special lunch party, some private event of our own.

Gradually in the other shops at Spring Valley I began to identify the owners. In the first of the *dukas* I found a Jenny-all-things shop similar to the one I had discovered in Glasgow, where among a miscellany of dusty items, one could discover a crusted silver vase, a rose bowl, a rare book. In the next shop, an elegant old Estonian with silver hair sold the best beef in Nairobi; in the next a green grocer; and in the largest, a general store, more or less everything.

It was here we met friends, made friends with neighbours, stopped to chat.

One day, there was no Amos. I asked the other flower-sellers. "Hospital," they said, shaking their heads. "He sick."

"Which hospital?"

They shook their heads again. "Very sick," they said.

I asked Mr. Lalvani, the paunchy General Stores owner perilously perched on a very small stool while he scrutinised every buyer.

"Gow'ment Hospital," he said.

That night when Alistair returned from work we drove out there taking Wachira with us in case of problems, and sent him in to enquire in which ward Amos was.

"No visitors," he said when he returned.

"Look," I said. "Tell them I am a doctor. I want to see him."

Wachira returned beaming. "Can go," he said. "I told them mama is Asian doctor."

Amos lay on a quiet bed on his own. Nearby a doctor stood writing on his pad.

"How is he?"

"Bad. Very sick."

"Does he have anyone – relations, friends - visiting him?"

"No, no one."

"I'll leave some money for him. Please- he's a good man." Then I went to Amos and bent over him.

"Amos –"

His good eye opened slowly. "Mama Wilson…"

"Get better soon, Amos. Remember your champagne roses. Others' not as good as yours."

"I get for Mama," he whispered.

I slipped some notes under his pillow, touched his hot, dry hand. "Amos, get well," I said. "I'll come tomorrow."

Next morning they told me he had passed away in his sleep.

In Nairobi fine new shops were mushrooming with bigger and better flower shops; new beauticians and hairdressers; fashion shops and general shops. The city with its surrounding hills and dales, its broad roads lined with jacaranda and other flowering trees, was spectacularly beautiful. Hotels and restaurants were doing well, it was a lovely city to be in, and we were truly happy.

Here there was always something new to learn, something new to do. At the Muthaiga Club, the food was superb, the Sunday lunches special. Now and then the few people left of the much written about Happy Valley crowd drifted in and out with a fence of privacy no one invaded. Now and then I would meet or see one or two of the famous ones, heard Mary Leakey and Joy Adamson lecture, and once saw Joy at a quiet wild life camp. I listened to the Leakey brothers lecture, twice saw Kuki Gallmann, close friend of our friends, but never spoken of. One did not trespass here. Except on wildlife territory.

❧

One drowsy afternoon the telephone rang.

A soft boy's voice with an English Public School accent asked, "Mrs. Wilson?"

"Yes,"

"Christine Wilson?" A slight hesitation, then, breathlessly, "Mrs. Wilson, I want to be your bedroom boy."

"What!"

"I want to be your slave. Your bedroom boy."

"Good gracious!" I said, playing along, "But I don't need a bedroom boy."

"Not for money."

This was beginning to be fun. "But you haven't even seen me!"

"I have."

"Where?"

"At the *duka*." This was getting closer to home now.

"How old are you?" I asked quietly.

"Sixteen,"

I took a deep breath. "Does your mother know you are doing this?"

A pause. "No."

"Look, my dear," I said, "I'm very flattered you phoned, but honestly, I don't think this is a good idea. Now would you forget that this conversation took place?"

There was a long silence. Then quietly the telephone went dead.

ôô

The first Christmas came and went. Wachira and George raided the forest for a ceiling-high, illicitly cut fir tree they decked with tinsel, lights, and balloons from the local *duka*. Christmas brought crisp sunshine, a snap in the night air, stars shining brighter than we had seen anywhere, and the moon a gilded melon.

For the long weekend in the New Year, we were offered a leave bungalow at the coast. Our first holiday since we had arrived, we happily packed looking forward to a visit from there to the Shimba hills, famous for its elephants and the rare Sable Antelope.

It was almost dusk when we arrived, the sea, sullen pewter, the bungalow unwelcoming with a surly cook in charge. However, with cameras and bags ready by our beds for an early start to the Shimba Hills, we were happy.

At about four in the morning Alistair awoke and yelled, "There's a man in the room!" Against the glass panes a dark shape moved. Simultaneously we dashed after him as he darted through to the sitting room, slithered thin as a snake through the glass slats of a window and disappeared.

Twenty minutes later the police with a guard dog appeared and listened to our story. One laboriously recorded it. The other two disappeared with the dog.

We sat at the double table dismally recounting our losses. Expensive new cameras, films, glasses, binoculars, a string of pearls I had forgotten to put away in Nairobi, and a pair of comfortable shorts Alistair dearly loved, had gone.

Towards dawn the search party returned. The dog had trailed the robbers, two of them, through thick undergrowth up to a road crossing, but lost the scent owing to a slight drizzle. They, however, had continued across the road and up a hill, where the loot had been sorted. "We recovered this," they said, triumphantly, and placed on the table Alistair's disreputable shorts.

At our house, the Nairobi police were busy too. Wachira had decided to practice his driving and had driven my Fiat 127 into the garage wall. We found him drunkenly asleep on the sitting room settee.

We kept him. The best, most loyal worker we ever had.

WE WENT TO THE Norfolk for a drink, and I sat folding and unfolding the cable Alistair had handed me. "Vera seriously ill with heart attack. Suggest Christine returns on visit." A doctor friend, Hamish Sproule, had sent it.

Traffic snarled around us. A Kikuyu waiter, red-capped, white-dressed, set coffee before me, a 'Tusker' for Alistair.

"I mean it," I said. "I've got to go back."

Other letters had come, hinting that things were not well at Wycherley. Whether I liked it or not, Wycherley was my responsibility. From the beginning I had been looked after, had had things done for me. This was something I had to do alone. Vera was more than family. As matron of my father's small nursing home she had been staunchly with us through bad times and good.

"Vera's devoted her whole life to us," I said. "I've got to go. Tomorrow if possible."

Alistair was staring at me.

"Go, then," he said. "Come on, let's get it over with and get your ticket."

Sitting in the plane I thought about nothing. It was going to be a strange day tomorrow. It was three years since I'd seen Wycherley. Abandoned it, as it stood, with all our things.

It was evening when I arrived, driven through the quick twilight that descends on my island. Friends met me, welcoming, expansive. I answered, staccato. "You've changed," they said. "Africa must be very beautiful." "Yes," I answered and was left at Wycherley.

Jane and Raman the manservant who looked after the dog met me, Jane crying. I too. For three years they had looked after this fully-furnished, lonely house for us. Were we mad to abandon it just as it was? No. Wycherley had developed a stranglehold on us, and the time was right. In the hall I touch the Dutch Bride-chest as I pass and catch a familiar snag in the mellow wood; overhead, the filigree copper lamp throws its pattern over the polished floor. Ahead, the stairway, sadly needing a new carpet. I go upstairs, hurting. Fourteen stairs to the small landing, seven to the next, larger one. The last eight with the one creaky step I had long ago avoided when I was out even a little late.

Then, the hardest part. Upstairs. Pictures. Books lining the walls. Rooms filled with memories. The bedroom is as we left it. My dresses in the wall-to-wall cupboard. On the old fashioned dressing table, the small Madonna figurine. On a dresser top, vases of garden flowers Jane has, as always, arranged for me. And standing stiffly, Barberton daisies she has bought. I start crying again.

This was not a good idea. I missed Alistair more than I could ever tell him. In Africa we had moved into a sphere of understanding in which Wycherley seemed far away. Then once again, as I had always done through the years, I ran downstairs and into Vera's room, to bury my head against her pale hand to weep for her and for my abandoned home.

"Christine?" she says in wonder, "I have been praying I would see you again."

"Now I'll get better," she said.

"You're not going to work in the nursing home any longer, darling Vera."

"Yes. It's a bit different from when your daddy and mummy were here. I'll be better, soon. You must go back now to Alistair."

"There are things to be seen to. Business."

"Alistair is more important," she said, and I nodded.

Alistair met me rather coldly. What had I expected? An ecstatic welcome after dashing off to Sri Lanka because Vera had had a heart attack? I put my hand, as I always did when we went driving together on his knee. It took a few seconds before he covered it with his own.

We turn in at our lane, past the double row of new, white or stone houses, and there is the forest, and the corner house, ours, snuggled in its lee. Before the locked iron-grilled gates we stop, and the headlamps shine on Stephen the guard opening it with a smiling salute, and by him in the flare of light, a strange creature.

"It isn't true!" I said. "What is it?"

"A welcome home present from Wachira," Alistair said. A dog he had found in the forest.

Its name was Bush: the most intelligent dog of all.

I HAD RETURNED TO my old love, painting in oils, and was absorbed in it when the telephone rang.

It was Vicki. "Hi!" I began when she cut me off quietly.

"Christine, Alistair's here –"

"What do you mean, 'here?'"

"At Nairobi hospital. No, listen. I'll collect you in a few minutes. Now don't panic. He's had a bit of a haemorrhage in the plane, he's on a drip, and he's going to be all right."

Between Dar-es-Salaam and Zambia he had haemorrhaged severely, staggered off the plane to his hotel and phoned his contacts to ask if his business meeting with them could be in his hotel room. A doctor checked and found his blood level had dropped alarmingly. But as the country at the time was in turmoil, and medical facilities bleak, he was advised to have his drip in Nairobi as soon as possible.

Incredibly he made his way alone to the plane; haemorrhaged again, arrived in Nairobi to be met by one of his colleagues, and rushed to hospital.

Vicki collected me and we dashed down to Nairobi hospital. Alistair lay white and drained, grinning a little lopsidedly as he saw me. "Been a bit of a bloody fool having this, haven't I?" he said.

I went over and held his hand. Icy cold. I peered at the bag pumping blood into my husband's body. Masai, it said.

"It's Masai blood," I said. Masai blood was fine, but there was much written in the newspapers at that time about *Green Monkey* though no one knew what it was about. I was suddenly alone in the room with my husband, and frightened.

"It's alright, Christine," I heard someone say.

But I was running down the long corridor to the Matron's desk. "They're giving him Masai blood!" I said.
She looked at me coldly. "So?"

"But why?" I blurted.

"There's nothing wrong with it," she said icily. "When someone's lost that amount of blood you have to be thankful for what you get. With the Pope's visit today, the blood bank's almost empty." It was the 3rd of March, 1980.

I phoned the office, and again it was Vicki, always ready to help. "Don't worry!" she said. Six of Alistair's friends arrived to give their blood.

It was not the end of the story. He was better, then, again, began a frightening undulant fever, 102, 103, plummeting down to subnormal. His white blood count was abnormally high and nothing would get it down.

I said quietly one day to Antonia Bagshaw the specialist who had now taken over Alistair's case, "He's very ill, isn't he?"

She looked at me. "Still fighting," she said. "If we can only get that white blood count down!"

The situation became critical. His illness could not be diagnosed. Meanwhile the lady in the next room who had been flown in from Uganda was cordoned off with a large notice saying, "Strictly no visitors." She died, it was whispered, of *Green Monkey*, which we who knew nothing called it.

Friends, acquaintances were more wonderful than ever. I had an open invitation to stay with friends near the hospital, or to have any meal, "Just drop in," they said. "Phone us at any time if you want us. We'll help in any way we can."

Alistair too, now had a 'Strictly No Visitors' sign outside his door.

I take my *petit-point* when I go to see him. Sit by the shaded window that hides sapphire skies and amethyst flowered jacaranda trees outside. From time to time I touch his hand, and there's a flicker of movement. "Guardie," I whisper, my special name for him. "Please get better."

"I will," the lips move.

"I counted twenty-two starlings' nests in our fever tree in the garden," I tell him on another day, and his eyes light up. We both love our garden and its birds.

"Bush and Honey send their special get-well love," I say every day. Our two Ridgebacks. "Please get well soon. They miss you, too."

He smiles. "I love them too," he says silently. His eyes speak.

The top specialist in the field now concentrates on Alistair's case. Antonia Bagshaw has a beautiful austere face that seems carved from ivory. I am a little scared of her. But one day after seeing him, I go up to her as she writes outside his room.

"Excuse me, Dr. Bagshaw. Please, how is Alistair?"

She looks up, and says, "For the first time there are signs of improvement."

"Thank you," I manage to say.

"It wasn't me we have to thank. Alistair's a fighter."

꙳

A while after, we had a party for all those who helped; the doctors came too and stayed till two in the morning.

WHEN THE RAIN CEASED at last, and spring began with its depthless blue skies and the purple mist of jacarandas, the owls came to us.

At six one morning, when Stephen, our Askari, came tapping at our window, pointing excitedly, we shoved on dressing gowns and hurried into the lower garden. High in the inglenook of the big double chimney, two large owls sat smugly side by side blinking sleepy eyelids at us.

Spotted Eagle owls! They'd come to nest.

In Sri Lanka we had a special affinity with owls. There was the seven-inch Scops owl that called in our Wycherley garden on moonlit nights; the *bimbussa*, or Ground owl of the jungles; and on the highest plains, the Forest Eagle owl screamed with the shrill cry of a woman being garrotted. But these, above our house, impressively large and beautifully marked, were obviously housekeeping. From time to time one or the other of them would lazily stretch and with a whoosh of wings fly towards the forest to feed on the small creatures there. For the rest of the day they were content to be gazed at by anyone who visited, though nothing much seemed to be happening.

One morning, between the two larger owls two small ones nestled. Friends flocked to see them, and our owls became famous.

They grew fast and the parents flew tirelessly back and forth into the forest to thrust food into the ravenous mouths.

"They're growing," Alistair said.

"Still fluffy," I said.

Once again Stephen the self-appointed guardian of the owls came knocking early at our window. But this time he looked worried.

"One small owl fall down," he said.

One of the youngsters deciding to fly had slithered down the sloping roof of our house and landed on the front porch. There it sat defiant with ruffled feathers and scarlet mouth open, daring us.

In the back garden, the three remaining owls sat expressionless in their chimneystack.

"Must carry and put where big owls are," said Nduati our gardener. Stephen shook his head. "Hawks will kill it. Better not to touch. Big owls will not come near if there is human smell."

Eventually Wachira suggested we put a dishcloth carefully over it, and carry it to the bushes at the base of the chimneystack. That night I lay awake thinking of a dozen different things that might happen to our owlet. Finally, I fell asleep knowing there was nothing more we could do.

Alistair woke me gently.

"It's dead? I know it's dead. Don't tell me."

"Come," he said, and took me to the window. On the great Mara tree facing the bedroom, the two parent owls sat smugly with the two fledglings between them.

Soon afterwards all four vanished. But a year later the male returned with another female. He was proud of his eerie, but she looked, pondered, and flew away, with him following more slowly.

ON A RAW SATURDAY afternoon, I drove Alistair home after a cataract operation. The garden, the whole hillside was wrapped in deep mist that sucked through the house and into our very being.

That night at 2:00am rocks thundered through our bedroom windows splintering glass into a myriad shards, on our beds, carpet, dressing table.

Alistair crept to the shattered window and peered through a chink in the curtain. "Bloody robbers," he said. My hand went automatically to the security bell behind our bed-head.
A voice spoke. "Security."

"Break in at Wilson's," I said, and gave our address. "Urgent. They're here."

"Coming. Stay in your security wing. Repeat. Stay in your security wing."

Alistair is at the window, whispering to Stephen our security guard who crept there. "Four," he whispers. "With guns and masks," and doubles back along the bushes. We could hear other windows being smashed along the length of the house. The scarlet figures of my bedside clock blink. 2:25am on this Sunday morning in September, one of the coldest months of the year. The cold seeps into the room and we, hurrying into dressing gowns and slippers, scrunch over shattered glass for torches. My torch throws frail light momentarily over Alistair's face with the dressing over his eye.

"They're in the house."

I nod in the darkness. An iron grill cuts our wing from the rest of the house, protects us. God knows for how long, if they have already broken through the grill of our sitting and dining rooms.

Leo, our African Ridgeback, was barking furiously. Then I heard a gunshot and silence.

"Dear God, they've killed Leo," I thought. Suddenly that seemed more real than the other things that were happening around us, sounds we could only guess at while the minutes ticked by. From time to time, Alistair disappeared down the long corridor to the grilled door, and returned looking grim. "They're in the sitting room." Time seemed eternal as we stood waiting, it seemed forever. For what, we did not know. Outside it was still dark with that absolute opacity I have only experienced in Kenya.

In the distance, then, we heard the sound of a vehicle approaching, stopping at our gate. Harsh voices shouted, feet thudded across the garden below our window. At last, a voice called, "You can come out of the safety area now."

I know now, the smell of evil. It filled the living rooms, foetid, irremovable. The sitting room was a wreck. Electric wires swung loose from the walls, two amplifiers lay on the floor by a photograph of my father, and another of Alistair smashed on the floor. In the dining room, drawers had been flung open their contents strewn, but time only for a Kashmir carving knife to be taken. They had broken through the iron grill with a cloth-covered arm thrust through a pane of glass to loosen a latch. Carefully selected electric equipment had gone.

·Outside a pallid dawn was breaking while we sat with the police taking statements, others running around taking fingerprints and busily powdering furniture in the hope of finding more. In the midst of this chaos I wander, still in my dressing gown, into the garden calling disconsolately "Leo!" but there is no answer, and the forest looks grim in that cold, raw, breaking dawn.

I returned to the sitting room. "I can't find Leo." No reply, so I went out again and walked in my slippers over the cold grass spiked with frost, out to the road to stare into the forest where the robbers had fled and left track marks of the vehicle in which they vanished with their loot, and called our dog again, but there was no silly mutt there to come running.

As we are each in turn being questioned, including the two security men, Alistair with his bandaged eye moved unruffled, speaking with authority to the men who surged round him, giving an order here, seeing to something there, Fixing me with an authoritative eye when I butted in with some irrelevant question.

"But where is Leo?" I asked.

He waved an impatient hand at me.

Leo was gone, and no one had any idea where. But Honey, his mate, quietly laid her head in my lap and whined softly, while outside the wind howled and the temperature hit a mean 12 degrees with the cold air driving through the empty windows.

Back at the house there were practicalities to be dealt with. The smashed windows needed to be patched quickly, but it was Sunday. With armloads of newspapers and tape they were dealt with. The police left and we set about bringing normalcy to our ravaged home with still no sign of Leo, which seemed the most desolating thing that had happened.

Rewards for Leo were tacked up in our provision store; we listened to people who swore they had seen him, once with a small black dog, another time wandering listlessly; someone else warned us that the "position is very dangerous, Mama. Peoples in this area eating dogs."

The whole situation was ridiculous. A bad break in, Alistair with his eye problem, this crazy intentness on finding a simple-minded dog that everyone loved.

One afternoon, five days later, John our cook came rushing to see me, "Mama, Mama, come, Leo is in the forest."

John had been sitting on the kerb outside our front gate, when he saw deep in the forest adjoining our house, a glimpse of Leo standing stock-still looking at him. He had called but Leo vanished.

He suggested, "We get Honey to call him." By now everyone had joined in the search. Hannah the garden lady took a broom in case of trouble. John, a slice of bread. I suggested we let Honey loose near where he had been, and there she made soft noises.

Presently he emerged, then gradually as he came closer, Honey nudged, licked him. Thin and disreputable-looking, his coat covered with burrs and ticks, at last the rake came home.

Alistair said wryly, "That darned dog got more attention than I did."

꙳

During our time in Kenya, I visited Lanka five times - Alistair three. The first, to get us out of the thraldom of leaving Wycherley vacant while the Nursing Home was still leased to others and leasing it instead to a school. The second on a four-month advisory term. Alistair's contract was extended, and extended again, and finally we decided to renew our lease and stay on – for how long we did not know.

A robber, capped with the usual black mask with slits for eyes was spotted by Stephen near our bedroom, and we decided. There was, after all, a house of our own waiting if we wanted it. But it was not Wycherley…

ALISTAIR HAD RETURNED FROM Tanzania almost voiceless. Now the last cigarette in the pack had set him coughing again, that harsh tearing sound I had heard so many times a day. He sat back in his chair exhausted.

"Darling, please, do something about that cough."
An irritable silence is broken by another spasm of coughing.

We were silent in the senior E.N.T. surgeon's consulting room at Nairobi Hospital as he held up the X-rays. "There's nothing much to be seen. But I think it would be wise, if you are going on leave soon, to consult the best E.N.T. man I know with a letter I'll give you."

Two weeks later in London as we sat in one of those quiet rooms down Harley Street, talking with a man in whose presence there was comfort, Alistair was given the all clear.

It was a clear June evening where people strolled in the Park, or sat at small tables dining off chequered tablecloths. Alistair and I were celebrating. He had passed all checks at hospital, the next day we were off to Washington, partly on business, partly to enjoy ourselves. When we returned to the club where we were staying, an urgent message awaited us. Would we return immediately to hospital at Mr. Grant's consulting rooms?

Alistair had cancer of the throat, they said. Further checks confirmed it.

"Go to Washington tomorrow as you planned," the surgeon said, "We'll deal with it when you return."

❧

On a day, cold, fogged with driving rain, we went by taxi looking at one service flat after another. I sat back in the taxi exhausted, while Alistair explored the last one. He returned, his face blurry against the misted window. "I've found one. Just right."

He dealt with his cancer in his own way. When he emerged from hospital he didn't want fussing or the indignity of being helped to dress or undress. It had to be his way, however long it took. Arrangements had already been made with his London office to have a quiet corner where he could work. The small apartment would have throttled him. When he returned from each treatment, exhausted, grey with pain, I learned silently to wait until he was ready to accept the liquid nourishment I mixed for him to sip through a straw, his face contorted. We communicated little, with me telling him the day's meagre news, reading him letters that came from all over the world, or what telephone calls had come asking how he was. If he had anything to say, he wrote it on a pad. There was no one in our small world except him and me, and great silences, in which we both tried to sleep when night came, but generally could not. Anne and Pia-Christina came from Denmark to visit him.

One night I phoned his eldest brother in Glasgow in tears. His wife came to the phone. "Elizabeth," I said and choked.

"Christine?"

"Jim, please."

When Alistair's brother came to the phone, his voice quiet, he asked, "How is he?"

"In such agony," I said, and the words blurred, "Please pray for him."

"We are, and thinking of him all the time. Keep strong, Christine."

At night he lies tensely awake. I watch, unable to help. He must fight alone, his way. Concentrate on this silent war within himself. "Let me help you, darling," I want to cry, but he cannot bear even the lightest pressure of my hand. I ask a question and he answers with a written word. Even to shake his head is too much. As the slow days pass, I try to form chaotic thoughts into prayer. "Dear God, make him better, let him be well. Tell me what I can do?" But how could I, who had not been to church for so long, ask now? What words could I find? I ask questions into the long night, and somehow, a prayer forms, which has no words. I touch the damp hand of my husband and whisper, "I love you, Guardie," and "Dear God – please make him better."

My husband survived a war in which his mother received a cable from him in Burma, and nothing for months. This was his other war. Finally he was given the all clear.

Alistair provided champagne for a small party on that last day at hospital when he was declared 'Clear'. The nurses, people in charge of the treatment unit, even the great surgeon himself was there and said, as Alistair thanked him, "We did the job. You helped get it right."

᪔

A letter arrived from New Zealand from friends who had been very close to us in Kenya. "Come," they suggested, "spend a homely Christmas and New Year with us in New Zealand and see in a happier New Year."

I look at photographs of that visit, and think "How lucky we have been," as I send up a wordless prayer of thanks. "How lucky I have been to have this good, strong, man as my husband."

I NEVER KNEW WHAT each day would bring. But always, some new experience.

Alistair and I sit on the veranda of our house in Colombo and talk about it, and there is a new lift to our voices. "Do you remember…? And the time …? No, it was the cheetah, at…" We are back at the beginning, in 1976.

We hired a small blue car, as we didn't have much money, and went to the Lake Manyara, the only place we saw lions resting on trees to get away from tsetse flies that tortured them. We saw a hammer kop's nest seven feet across, a herd of elephants came up to us, not thirty feet from our tent.

In the rented Volkswagen Beetle we drove to the Ngorongoro Crater in Tanzania and back. Seronera camp. "Remember the black maned lions? And the Kopji where a single lion lay majestically. And you suggested we switch seats and you move in, while I went round the car and got devoured by the lion?" We laugh again.

There is so much to remember.

Endless miles of straight roads and open spaces where dust devils rose and swirled and went dancing away. Hot tarmac bubbled and our tyres exploded. Driving out to the coast in the new Mazda 929, Alistair was hitting 120 when the tyres burst. The car juddered left, right, left again and landed nose up in a ditch in the middle of scrub, lion country, with not a vehicle in sight. Neither of us spoke. Alistair edged out of the half fallen car and walked round to inspect the damage. "You have a spare tyre?" I asked. He sucked on his pipe. "A flat one. Two of ours burst just now."

"Have some chocolate," I suggested. He took it automatically. "Lion country," I observed looking around for any sign of habitation.

A long time later, a happy crowd of Africans came singing down that empty road in a small Citroen. "What's the trouble, Bwana? Can we help?" They suggested I could drive with them to Mombasa and return with tyres and a mechanic in a hired car to collect Alistair. It was a holiday weekend and the chances of getting anything done were gloomy. So off I went and it seemed a long time later when I returned. He was smoking his pipe and ruminating. Our African friends said, "There's a sisal farm near here; let us drive you there and see if they can help."

The owner was a Greek, Nikko Geovardis. Immediately he sent two of his men in a tractor to tow the car back to the ranch, and meanwhile suggested a meal and a room for the night.

It was a gracious, typically Kenyan house with zebra rugs on the floors, leopard skins thrown over settees, mounted animal heads on the walls. Anna his wife, (one was immediately on first-name terms with people in Kenya) was a slim, rangy beauty in riding breeches. When she came in from the stables she was as welcoming as her husband. It was the sort of hospitality that we found everywhere in the Africa we knew.

Alistair's Parish covered Kenya, Uganda, Tanzania, Mauritius, Lesotho, Ethiopia, Malawi, Sudan and Somalia. He travelled with a team generally, and only occasionally could I go with him, keeping a low profile. We visited far places, saw lands of mountains, chasms, waterfalls, mist, storms, craters, and snow-topped mountains, deserts and forests so thick we never knew when we would be charged by a vast elephant with fanned-out ears breaking through the green, trumpeting. A boy sits on a hillside chipping at a piece of wood with a pocket-knife. "What are you making?" we ask, they all know English. He answers, "A gazelle passed this way and I thought I would make him in wood." He holds it out to us. "For you, take," he said. "Not for money."

One Sunday in Mauritius we drove out to see a hill of seven layers of different coloured sand. Along the way we met a group of youngsters dancing barefooted, to the music of a guitar, and stopped to take a photograph. "Come, join us," they said. I kicked off my shoes, linked arms and danced along.

Kigali… le pays de mille collines…The land of a thousand hills. Friends took me to visit the wildlife park there. At the entrance is a large board on which is pinned a dozen enlarged photographs under the title 'The Animals Here are Wild.' The first photograph shows half a dozen white safari wagons parked around some lion cubs. They focus in on a single auto. A man is getting out of it. He leans close to the cubs. There is a close-up of a large lion, a lions paw descending, next the face of the woman in the car screaming, her mouth wide open. The paw descends…

≈

At the Mara, our favourite Park, we saw early in the morning a frieze of elephants on a ridge, silhouetted against a dawn sky. Alone in the centre stood a single elephant, a dark bundle at her feet. The driver trained his binoculars on her, then quietly drove closer. "New-born elephant," he said. "Something wrong." He edged closer still until the mother lifted a warning trunk. "Let her be," he muttered and drove rapidly away not answering our questions.

On our afternoon drive he went there again. The female elephant still stood there, but the rest had moved a little. Without speaking, Stephan handed me his binoculars. "The baby is deformed," he said. As I looked I saw the baby weakly trying to move a crippled limb.

Next morning the frieze of elephants had gone, the mother slowly disappearing over the crest of the hill leaving an empty plain.

॰ॐ॰

We now went for unusual sights, not just the endless herds of elephants, though we always loved them but something beyond which was the heart of those parks. One evening we came upon an ostrich sitting on a cluster of eggs. It rose and we counted 36 eggs. It was possible that it may have been laid there by another bird and it was the father who was sitting there.

We visited the Mara again with the same tracker, now our friend. He drove us silently for a long time, almost boringly long with nothing but the familiar types; the buffalo, a lion or two, a fish eagle on a bare branch. We drove along the plain to a further part of the Mara, with no elephants, cheetahs, leopards anywhere in sight. He stops, binoculars at his eyes, drives on. What did you see? We ask. He does not answer, but drives on steadily; then into sight come a phalanx of eight ostriches flanked on either side by the mother and father and between them the youngsters. Eight of them. Running, half-flying towards us at amazing speed. With outspread wings and wide-open beaks they charged our vehicle. "Put your window up!" I heard as I snapped a picture of a red open maw and a smear of black wings against the glass of the window.

॰ॐ॰

Back in Nairobi, I am completely happy, because I have found things to learn, which is, to me one of the most important parts of my life. There was so much unlearned, untapped, before. I am a sucker for suggestions.

"Why don't you join the Vera Brablik School of Dressmaking and Tailoring?" I am asked. Yes, why not? Two years later I come out of it with two dresses; a smart red suit with slacks, an alternative skirt, waistcoat and a tailored jacket. "Why don't you just go out and *buy* some good clothes," Alistair suggests. Maybe dressmaking was not my forte.

"Why don't you join oil-painting classes?" someone asks. Why not? I adore the smell of turps, the slither of paint. "But I don't know how to get the feel of this rain-drowned garden," I plead with my teacher. She looks at it, ponders, sees my hopeful look. "Try," she says moving on. The picture sold. I studied Flower arranging. Satisfying, but I was not for rules, my spirit still searches, must run free. Back to oil painting with Keith Harrington. "Yes!" I say, remembering my painting under the guidance of Donald Ramanayake in Colombo. There is so much more to learn. I love the smell of paint, the vast horizons of this lovely land. But I discover I can't draw perspectives, my Moorish houses of Zanzibar lean in the wrong direction. The lonely river I enjoyed painting is no different. I am asked by Princess Didi, "My dear, how come your river is running uphill?" and indeed it was in my picture, I found, as I glanced furtively at it on the wall behind my desk.

Let me return to my wild lands. Flamingos pink and grey walk on stilt like legs in their saline mud-flats, rising in a raucous cloud without notice of their going; a leopard at a kill looks straight at me, keen eyes topaz.

I paint on porcelain now, and it became a lasting passion. Alistair and I are happy. Happier than we have ever been in our lives. His life is full of freedom to achieve in the ancient lands of East Africa. Dream names of Tanzania, Uganda, the Blue Mountains, Ethiopia, Mauritius. He has helped create the new tea factories. We have found together new places, new interests, things to do. I too, have dreams come true and the freedom to explore.

It was nearly midnight. In the centre of the clearing a log fire roared, throwing sparks of flame. Firelight touched the circle of intent people, waiting.

There is no other sound but the wind in the trees and the fire. Then, out of the quiet comes the deep-throated voice of the people of the Mara. First, the drumbeat of bare feet, stamping step by evocative step forward. Plumed and painted warriors advance with spears, with each step uttering a deep-throated Ugh! Ugh! Firelight touches the whites of eyes, a warrior's cheekbones, gleaming bodies. One warrior after another jumps high with upheld spears, the next higher. Pushing past tourists the line thrusts forward into the space around the fire for this is their night. This, their land. I watch, hypnotised, behind them, women and young girls with oiled and near-nude breasts pressed close against the back of the woman ahead. The men jump higher, lust in their eyes; the women aware, tongues ululating, bodies wet with perspiration. Then a bouquet of fireworks bursts into the sky exploding, and a great cry breaks out. A fire balloon rises, more fireworks. Suddenly it is the New Year, with the smell of Africa strong in this new dawn.

Alistair and I picked up our torches, and I my stole, for the night air was sharp as we edged away from the crowd to our tent. By the dark path dimly lit at intervals by hurricane lamps, an Askari waited to conduct people to their tents overlooking the river. On the other side of the path, the dark forest. A sudden movement in the trees, and the Askari pushed me urgently off the path and gestured to Alistair. A few yards ahead a massive tusker with impressive tusks advanced out of the gloom, trunk raised, walked slowly down the path past us, and out of sight. Elephants have right of way, is the unwritten law of these national parks. This one, the guard knew as the camp elephant, which often foraged the food bins. But this night it was uneasy with the noise and flare of fireworks. Sometimes others wandered down here, the Askari added casually. He carried no weapon but his baton and a torch.

We sat for a while in the canvas-covered veranda area, watching the river as we had done at intervals for nearly twenty years, waiting for the splash that tells us of hippo, slithering down the opposite high bank to bathe; sometimes an elephant or two, a herd of bush buck.

"It's perfect, isn't it? I said to Alistair. He nodded. His voice would always be throaty, but that was unimportant.

The stars, the moon always seemed brighter here than elsewhere.

Now it was cloudless, perfect.

"Happy New Year, darling," I said again. My voice, too, a little husky this time. Our hands gripped. Then suddenly from the tree in front of our tent there broke out the most horrendous screaming. Like the frantic crying of a child.

"What the devil -?"

He was outside, his torch flaring.

"Come! Look at this," he said.

Torchlight shone on two terrified globular eyes shining out of the neck of what looked like a jam bottle. One skinny arm with a black, kid-glove hand clung to a branch. Inside a jam bottle a small loris-like creature was trapped.

This was the nocturnal creature that at night filled the forest with his banshee cries. A Bush-Baby. It looked at us piteously, but we could think of no way of getting it out. I called the Askari who was gentle and knew what to do. He reached for it expertly, and soon it was out and away and up into the high branches of trees far out of sight.

This often happened, the Askari said indulgently, "He *too* much liking jam." We had come to love the little creatures which, belonging to the family of monkeys and lemurs curled up asleep during the day, and hit the night with diabolical shrieks as they swung through the branches unseen. In Sri Lanka we had their kin, the slender loris. I once saw a Vedda with the most rare and beautiful of its kind, a golden loris, over his shoulder.

I love the Mara, I thought. It is unending in its surprises.

We went there every New Year's Eve now. To spend it anywhere else in Africa seemed unthinkable.

We did not know that this was to be the last time.

෨

The people there now knew us, and we, them. The men who drove the safari vehicles, a proud lot, accepted us as safari people. Like homing pigeons we went to the same tent, Number 25, on the high bank above the river where every sound meant something.

On New Year's day we drove out at six, with a more sleepy driver than usual, for a sight of great plains, the new dawn breaking red-gold and amethyst over the horizon, and the feeling that the New Year was well begun.

I who had spent some of the best times of my life in Sri Lanka's jungles, felt small against this vastness. In Africa, I had to learn the rules of an at first unfamiliar territory; new ways of understanding the unwritten law of the wild that existed in this vast country, one of whose parks could hold my entire island. We learned slowly, humbly, through lectures by Mary Leakey and her sons the Leakey brothers, reading books by experts of whom we sometimes had a sighting in a Park as they drove past, or waited in secret places with binoculars watching leopard, or whatever creature in which they specialised. Once we met Cynthia Moss whose passion was elephants. She sat, a gentle woman, not young, not old, under a flap of her tent, writing, her notebook on her knee. Round her a small group of elephants nudged each other for the fruit of a tree near her tent. The drivers knew and respected the writers who wrote with passion about their wildlife, and usually only vaguely pointed towards their camps as we passed quietly, not to disturb them. 'Joy Adamson's camp, or, Cynthia Moss typing while elephants nibbled around her.' But there were, at times, glimpses of them in a Nairobi bookshop, at a hotel function. Very occasionally, a chance meeting in a park.

When we were new here, we left it to the drivers to take us where they would. Sometimes they asked what would we like to see? In the beginning it was lion hunting - cheetah, leopard. Later "Wherever you would like to take us." If we were fussing too long over baby lions, one of the drivers would patiently read his bird book, with an occasional look out for the mother. His proud duty was to see that visitors however raw, however experienced, saw what they wanted to and were happy. At last we said, when we knew them well enough, "Take us to whatever interests you." "Everything interests us," one replied. "Some things more than others." Gradually we won their confidence. We were more than tourists. In time we would drive far from the tourist routes for endless miles to far places where there seemed to be only hills and the odd herd of buffalo, a vulturine eagle on a dead tree; a giraffe peering inquisitively, lions we passed barely stopping to photograph them.

Then there would be something special. Once we watched a baby impala being born. It took twenty minutes until the fawn struggled to its feet and, nudged by its mother, began to suckle. On one of our first safaris we stopped to see the rare hunting dogs, but never saw them again for rabies wiped them out.

Relatively unafraid of elephants, we sat within feet of them as they and their youngsters ambled around us. We watched them break whole trees, nibble a frond or two, casting the rest aside, destroying their sustenance. Dead areas with skeleton trees revealed the damage done. These drivers knew within a foot or two how close they could get, so close we could see the grain of ivory in tusks larger than I had ever imagined.

Leopards were the hardest to see. Again and again we visited a rocky cliff, the haunt of leopard we never saw. But we found a young gazelle so badly wounded by leopard, that the tracker sprang out of the vehicle to examine its wounds. "Leopard!" he said switching on the engine roughly. "Hopefully it will die soon before the buzzards and jackals get it."

As we stayed longer and longer we fused into the pattern of these parks of East Africa, so different from those in Sri Lanka. I tried to sketch, but could not. There was too much to watch. I did not keep a diary - perhaps because there was too much to record, too much feeling I could not express on paper. Now I must rely on memory alone, which registers colours, particular sounds, some almost beyond the range of hearing, some startlingly resonant: the trumpeting of an enraged Ugandan elephant, that charged us in a track so narrow we could only reverse madly. The hoarse squawk-squawk of rose-pink flamingos in the salterns; slithery-grey backs of eighty three close-packed hippos, grunting, rumbling, snorting, blowing, snapping, in their oozy shallows in Uganda; beyond them, on a knoll, a pride of fourteen lazy lion.

Anne on safari with us in Kenya

I have picture-memories of giant crocodiles, scarlet maws gaping; packed buffalo herds heading in a mad rush for water; rhino, white ox-pickers on their backs; moments of drama; moments of peace when we saw nothing, but did not mind. The thrill of seeing, for the first time, a few feet from our vehicle a bouquet of sun-gilt lion and their young, the cubs chasing each other, biting a tail here, a flank there until a low growl from the lioness brings them trotting back to her. In Serengeti, three baby cheetah walked unafraid towards our vehicle, stood close against a wheel, stared up at me and snarled as I snapped them. A flash later the mother charged towards her siblings, and they trotted away behind her.

In the Christmas/New Year of 1982/83 when the frontier between the two countries had just opened there was that strange visit to Tanzania, with Alistair, I, and four friends — the first to cross the closed border in years. The country, we were warned, was desperately short of necessities, so, filling our vehicles with a dozen electric bulbs, soap, and whatever else we could think up including Christmas crackers, gifts, and Christmas fare, we set out.

What we had heard was true. At the safari lodge cobwebs hung from the eaves; water ran in a dispirited trickle into rusted baths; there was no soap, no toilet paper; a shortage of electric light bulbs. There was a petrol shortage (fortunately we had brought plenty); and no liquor; (this too we brought, plus everything for a Christmassy Christmas especially for the two youngsters.)

In two Land Rovers six of us drove over the border into a different East Africa. We saw three cheetahs flattened in a coppice. A shifting breeze; heads rise uneasily; slowly the cluster begins to scatter as out of a thicket something moves. The herd begin their panic run across the plain; a streak of yellow quickens pace towards the flying hooves, a youngster breaks out too far and the final chase is swift. The cheetah's outstretched body is beautiful in this final taut-muscled attack, the slashing paw, and... - but I cannot look, though it is part of the whole of which we are a part.

Driving back I asked Alistair, "What is it, I wonder, that makes us nature lovers, even begin to watch a kill with such fascination?" I felt it was a privacy invaded. Or was it an honour to let us share through this a better understanding of nature and how it exists, lives and dies?

"To witness what is part of life and death in nature," he answered, "is a privilege, part of a cycle that helps us understand our own lives."

"But I've seen excitement in the eyes of those watching."

"I'm hungry," he said, and would say no more. It was Christmas Eve.

We were the only foreigners at the lodge. They had made a brave effort to decorate the room with the coloured tissue-paper we had brought. They had blown up the balloons, placed Christmas crackers on the table, gifts. The lodge had made an effort to serve the best meal they could from what was available. We had brought the Christmas pudding, the mince pies. Then the crackers were pulled, streamers thrown across the room to include the other diners, whistles blown, and jokes in the Christmas crackers read.

❧

Back in Kenya, we went at another Christmas-time, to Governor's Camp in the Masai Mara.

When we returned exhausted from the morning run there was the magnificent Mara breakfast in the open. Elephants wandered on the edge of the plains; from the Mara river came the splash of a hippo. Anything was possible and it was good to be alive and there.

❧

From our Nairobi terrace I look on the cherry tree that years ago George planted, in full bloom now; and also, something I have never seen before, two karrapinchcha-leaf (curry-leaf) trees I had brought from Lanka, eight feet high here, and mantled with small pale yellow flowers.

The time for our departure is close. I look back. Look forward into the present, but that I cannot see. I know too little of the wars that have split my island asunder. How would they and we react with each other? I did not know. But the jungles will still be there, I said. And the birds, the call of the peacock...

One more visit to the Mara, please, I say.

My first time there I saw a cheetah kill in one hunting session, three impala. On that last morning, it was fitting that we should chance on cheetah yet again. Leaving camp at dawn, the sun blinding our eyes as it slowly cleared the rim of the plain, then on and on, until we came at last to a place we had never been to before. Ahead, plains rolled away into the now-glowing sunrise. It had drizzled last night, and now, at the horizon we saw a rainbow appear. Then, in the foreground, an anthill, and on it a cheetah in all her beauty, sitting proud towards the sun; below her, four cubs gambolled. We take the memory like a good luck charm with us. Beauty and grace and happiness were there. Whatever lay ahead could not dim that memory.

TO RETURN OR NOT to return? The question lay heavily on our minds. We had been in Sri Lanka for our fiftieth wedding anniversary and been blessed in the Scots Kirk church where we married. "Come back, come back," our friends said. Maybe it was time.

We each kept a notebook. Each day we wrote plus or minus points in two columns. Every time we passed the Spring Valley brook below our road we were freshly enchanted. Every time we returned from a dinner party to find our house, the whole of our lane in the menace of another unannounced electricity cut, we'd fumble to unlock doors, search for torches, light lamps, stumble to our room, and decide this was too much.

There was a peculiar sombreness about those blackouts when thieves roamed and no one knew what appalling things were happening. But when we woke to dew-fresh dawns filled with bird song and a tune in the wind, it was different. In the garden, Nduati busily prunes a triple-flowering bougainvillea into a leafy tea-bush shape that would never flower. Leo and Honey, the golden Ridgebacks, follow my amble through the garden, stopping to look at a rose here, a gardenia there. Leo, sensuously rubs his back under a trailing scratchy bougainvillea stalk. The fever-tree in the centre of the lawn is hung with the twenty-two forgotten nests of the weaverbirds that nested there in a year of crisis. The chimneystack where the two Forest Owls perched with their two youngsters is empty. Maybe they'll return next year? But then Wachira our cook, comes demanding his rights, the usual three weeks' leave. Alistair is suddenly in a foul temper. I retire to my study to do some porcelain-painting, create a web of butterflies over the snow of a porcelain plate. Then, restless with the thoughts underlying all I do now, I go outside pick an armful of roses; shoo away two monkeys who have stripped a bed of golden corn cobs in the vegetable garden which is lush with tomatoes, peas, beans, rosemary, basil, thyme.

Memories surge back. I am seated under a mango tree at Wycherley with my ayah cooking my first curry over a three-brick fire. Later I would offer to my parents on miniature Dresden plates, rice, and a dish of potato curry. First, my father, then my mother. Other memories follow. Jungles. Heat. Beaches. Mosquitoes. Friends. The friends, who like me, will have made other friends now. Wycherley, which is a school now.

Every evening Rosemarie my German friend, phones me or I phone her, to say Hello. I would miss people like Rosemarie and others who for four years had studied Porcelain painting with me, shared safaris, and visited each other's homes regularly.

Yes, I would miss my friends of twenty years, knew it would be harder to make new friends, re-establish old ones, even Lankan friends of a lifetime with whom, before, we had shared memories.

I run to meet Alistair when he returns from work and we sit close on the terrace veranda. The small cherry George planted twenty one years ago has given up its fight against wild mistletoe, but it bears two gallant flowers. I feel a heart-jerk of foreknowledge that we would leave this place of forests, wild-lands, mountains and friendship.

Unexpectedly the question arises: "What would my father have said if he were alive?" The question remained unanswered, but later I woke as if he had spoken. He would have said out of his great knowledge, "The choice is yours. But remember wherever you've been, whatever you do, there are halls of gold in our island.

Remember the vast cave in our forests, large enough to house a cohort of soldiers, and inscribed with the ancient Pali words, 'To Tissa beloved of the gods'. Remember, a great rock-hewn swimming pool, with a cobalt reflection of the sky. I remember things the present generation has never seen, but you have. Delft Island, with wild ponies galloping with wind-tossed manes. Caves, then unexplored, which you climbed over rocks and creepers to see? You, who have been blessed to see more than most people, how can you turn your back on what is your heritage, and part too, of Alistair's, now?"

I turn to my husband. "How does our tally go today?" "Look at the thunderheads piling," he said. I answered, "I see Aeolious god of the wind in that frowning cloud. Listen to the song of the wind." I fling down my notebook. "Oh God, it shouldn't be this difficult."

❧

We came at last to our home in Sri Lanka with our suitcases. Crates to be opened surrounded us. Only kitchen equipment had been unpacked and arranged in cupboards by our new maid.

There were two beds in the bedroom we had selected as ours. No mirror; no cupboards or other furniture. We ate by candlelight, for there was, ironically, a total electricity and water cut that lasted three days. The temperature was hitting the 40s.

As we sat down at a small candle lit bridge table to eat, we looked at each other and burst out laughing. I lifted a glass of wine and said to my husband, "Welcome home."

❧

During our twenty years away the island had changed. Spoken English was being swallowed by Sinhala. The charming small politeness had disappeared and a proud new people had emerged who learned English in their sixth form. But our staff were of the old school.

Our favourite, perhaps, was Aideen. Small-made, with two front teeth missing, he wore his green sentry suit with pride and had the friendliest smile.

"I'll pay for new teeth," I said. His grin grew wider. No way, it seemed to say, most courteously.

He approached us quietly as we stood washed in the early moonlight of our first evening, and pointed. On a branch of a flowering tree two small Scops owls softly called as long ago other owls had called in that other tree in Wycherley across the way.

I asked him what jungly creatures we had; a mongoose, he said, which was good to keep down snakes; two sedate monitor lizards sometimes crossed our lawn; a yellow wild cat, even a monkey who later seated on our wall, took a banana from my hand. There were pole cats in the roof, squirrels nesting indoors and out and snakes, but they would not worry us. Yet one day, through the trellis of our indoor courtyard, a snake slithered through the dining room and into the garden chased by Jenny, our dog. Our house-girl Kamala, swore there was a dangerous maapilla not far from her kitchen. But she was given to hysteria.

Soon Aideen became our friend. We spoke with him on jungle matters, plants, birds and such, and he always knew the answer. On bleak days he could still find some treat. He brought me strange wind-blown seeds frail as cobwebs; showed me the turquoise, brown-speckled eggs of a tailor bird in a nest of leaves stitched with gossamer. He would watch with Alistair and me at sunset, parrots flying in green skeins over a gold and crimson sky, then crows, and finally bats, maybe a thousand of them moving unerringly to roosts far away.

But special were our talks about the *Ruk-Athana* tree. At Wycherley long ago a dropped seed from some distant jungle had taken root and grown. Every part of it, from crown to roots, my father told me, was used; some for medicinal purposes. Now, its sibling was here, like us grown old, yet full of youth's joy at small things. Now a kingfisher - a flash of turquoise; the Paradise Flycatcher with a streamer of white. A skein of green parrots screeching overhead.

Every evening towards dusk, Aideen lit a few sticks of incense, rhythmically wafted till their fragrance rose as far as the patio where we sat to watch the moon rise over the trees.

He came from a quiet coastal hamlet beyond Tissamaharama, knew all the wild places I had known long ago; the plants, animals, birds, reptiles. He knew ancient stories, now almost forgotten.

The owls continued to be our favourite birds, for there was love and nostalgia in their wooing; but this year they had not come. Or rather, he said, they came at about four in the morning, "and I cannot call Sir or Madam then," he said. His smile contained even more gaps than before.

"Aideen," I said, "I have advised you not to keep having these teeth extracted. Not replacing them is no good for you. I have told you I will pay for new ones."

He went away that evening on three days leave to his village down south where he was building a small house for his unmarried sister. He was a loner who never married.

At five o'clock next morning they phoned to say he was dead. He had eaten a good dinner and gone to bed. At midnight he complained of pain in his chest and was taken by lorry to hospital. An hour later he passed away from a massive heart attack of which there had been no warning.

&

It was a Sunday and the usually busy main road was quiet. Everyone was quiet that day. But as I moved around the house I became aware of a strong, remembered scent, and as the day grew, it grew stronger. That evening I stood on the veranda and thought about it, then went round to the side of the house along a strip of garden no more than a passage large enough for three large trees set against a neighbouring wall.

Rising above the others our *Ruk-Athana* tree spread wide, mantled with small, creamy-green, scented flowers. All night flowers fell over the red tiles of our roof, the drive and the next-door garden. Suddenly I thought of Aideen who at about this time lit his incense sticks. He had always run to tell me when the flowers came.

Next day the scent was overpowering. Now over the flowers clouds of butterflies flew, yellow, dark grey and blue, and above, black screeching crows arrived with beating wings from all around to feast off butterflies. Alistair joined me, and as we stood amazed, flowers drifted over us. Crow-driven butterflies scattered, some drunkenly wheeling over flower beds, others indoors to cling to walls and ceilings. On our veranda alone I counted over a hundred, all the colour of pale smoke, with deeper dots scalloping their wings; the yellows and blues outside, wheeling, falling.

The staff came and looked at each other, wondering. Kamala, the house maid broke into loud sobs.

For three days the flowers lay heavy under the tree. Inside the house, the butterflies still plastered the walls until they fell; outside, the others had vanished.

"It's a seasonal flower," Alistair said. "It's well known that all over the island certain species flower at the same time."

I looked at a younger *Ruk-Athana* tree half hidden by the tall Indian Cypresses along the front wall of the garden. No flowers there. I looked across the road at the Wycherley tree that still stood high. No flowers there either. But near our sentry box, an *Ehela* tree, out of season, produced a single spray of pale yellow flowers. That one spray and no more.

I have no explanation to offer.

꙳

I began to search for my island, but much of it had changed. Wilpattu game sanctuary which I had loved more than any had been violated and was still in the hands of Tigers. In the city, walls had grown high, hiding from the openness of the friendly houses I had known. I missed our beloved dogs that we had left staring reproachfully after our car as we left. We had always had dogs.

Around six one evening we heard a commotion at the gate. There stood our driver Wilbert with a club in his raised hand. Shrieks from our housemaid of *"Balla maranda"* - kill the dog! Wilbert stood with a club raised in his hand, and a crumpled pink bag of polythene on the ground.

"What's going on?" I called as I heard a puppy piteously crying. A very small pup off the roads had been thrown through our gate in a plastic bag, "No good dog, this, Madam, having rabies maybe, must kill," Wilbert shouted raising his stick again.

"No one kills any animal in this house," I said almost running down the drive. "Let me see it," A tiny pup black with mange that left her minus hair on her body lay there helplessly. Two piteous eyes stared at me out of a small, unmistakably no-account street dog's face. We had our first dog.

Trembling with rage now, I ordered warm milk in a saucer. Asked the sentry to keep it safe until we could take it to the vet next morning.

"What's her name?" asked the vet. "Jimmy," I said.

"It's a her." Then, "Jenny," we said, and so Jenny entered our lives.

She was a little yellow dog, a pure Sinhala hound with a regular upturned tail and bright intelligent eyes. I had always wanted one, and this one off the streets (where four or five of her brothers and sisters were born) was fine, for she had found us. Her treatment at the vet's continued daily until gradually her coat grew. She was spayed and became the most gallant canine patient I have known. The morning after her operation she jumped onto my bed and slept so peacefully I let her lie. She adored Aideen the sentry, Wilbert, who was now her good friend, me and Alistair in that order. At a word from us she'd come racing along the lawn and onto our laps. We bought her a collar (soon discarded) – a Sinhala hound must run free - special pet food, pet shampoo, and she was ours. A small dog that loved deeply, and was an excellent protector against strangers.

∼

A friend who revered my father visited last evening. He had grown thin, and white locks lay on his neck. He came to present the gift of his latest book, *Ruhuna's Heritage* about jungle country he, my father and I had known well. He had been a junior employee of the great Mahaveli River Development Scheme when thousands of acres of primary forests were felled to make way for a vast irrigation scheme. Its inhabitants fled before the tide of the swollen river, the Jungle people, the Veddas, hurried like scared children from their secret hideouts. Where could they go? How could they, food gatherers who trapped or hunted, find sustenance outside their forests? Our friend Gamini Punchihewa knew them well. After my father's death he took over the crusade of the Veddas and their territory, and visited Alistair and me from time to time to talk about forgotten things.

The early Vedda's great-grandchildren still lived where government had settled them. When, after twenty and a half years in Kenya we returned, I could no longer visit them. I always asked Gamini how they were.

"Still yearning for their lost identity," he said.

But this was not entirely what he came to talk about. "How is it," he asked gravely after three quarters of an hour of reminiscing, "there is so little mention of your mother in your book about your father?[1] She lived, she died..." his voice trailed off in a question mark. I noticed he had taken off his sandals and rested one of his crossed feet above the other.

I looked away. "He - my father had just died," I said. Typically he died with the clarion call of the jungle fowl in the aviary calling. Typically there was that last touch of the Vedda, who, somehow had travelled far, I do not know how, to mourn under a tree in the Wycherley garden, then to come into the house and in front of David Paynter's lovely life-sized panting of him, sing his song to the new dead – which I taped and later lent, and never received back.

[1] *Surgeon of the Wilderness*

"But so little about your mother," Gamini persisted looking gravely at me.

My mother had lived on speechless, paralysed in the nursing home for four incredible years from 1948 to '52. She passed away so quietly, we who had loved her were glad for her sake. "She was one of the finest people I ever knew," I said.

"How, then, was she not included more in this book?"

He was right to ask Why? *Why?* She deserved a book in her own right for I owed her more than I could ever express. And now there was no time left.

Before he left I asked Gamini if he would sing a Vedda lullaby for my mind was in turmoil. He looked gravely at me, then putting down his brief-case, folded his hands and rocking gently began softly to sing while I sat mesmerized, remembering as if it was now, a little girl whose mother sang "Baby, Baby Bunting, Daddy's gone a-hunting to get a little rabbit skin to wrap the baby Bunting in…"

Gamini went away quietly, treading the gravel drive with careful feet and down-bent head, his knapsack over his shoulder. I sat in the darkening veranda staring across at the house on the other side of the road where my mother, father and I had had our home, and it is she who floods my mind.

"Bunting, darling, like to come shopping with me to buy Christmas presents?" Her voice is soft, crystal clear. "Like to go afterwards to Cave's tea rooms for an ice cream?"

The Pettah was hot, but it was fun skipping along covered pavements busy with ladies with parasols, long, belted dresses and high-heeled shoes.

My mother bought carefully thought-out presents for all my father's nephews and nieces. Tirelessly gift-wrapped parcels for the children who, grown elderly, now, still remember how much they had looked forward to her presents.

∾

My mother is dressing for a formal dinner party at Wycherley. The long mirror of her dressing table throws back her reflection as I watch: her hair softly pinned, brushed with a silver brush engraved with her initials, C.F.v.D. She wears formal black lace and pearls for the party downstairs where she will be the perfect hostess while her husband holds guests riveted with his conversation. Time passes.

An urgent call comes from the operating theatre of the Wycherley nursing home, and my mother is down there, scrubbed up, capped and gowned to anaesthetize for my father while he operates on an emergency case. "The best anaesthetist I ever had," he says afterwards.

I grow, aware that my life was divided. The little girl of the frilled party dresses and perfect manners is also the rebellious one, encouraged by my father who seeks in me the son he never had.

It was becoming a clash between my parents, who talk about me when I have gone to bed, at odd moments during the day, for they were equally obsessed with this only-child syndrome. My mother wanted to bring me up 'properly' in the Cheltenham College way, well mannered, gentle; my father said, 'No!' He wanted me to run free, yet when later I want to run free, he is the parent most disturbed.

"Never talk to strangers," she'd say repeatedly. Now I love talking with anyone I meet. There's a wealth of people out there and I reach out to them.

When my mother entered her stroke the last thing she managed to utter was, "Darling, I have never been able to tell you how much I love you."

No, I still cannot write about my mother, Gamini. Just as she couldn't talk about herself, or emotions, ever.

I had few people left in the family now. Anne her husband and daughter are in Denmark. Although we phone or e-mail almost daily, for the first time I asked myself "Where do I belong?"

❧

I have found that I can let my mind drift now here, now there, lingering over what was good, and there was much good; slurring over the bad times, for there is no purpose in recalling them. It is a time for thought, and thanks for all that was best in the past, not a time for recrimination, for what cannot be cured now.

Remember jumping unseen in the monsoon rain when I was eight? Remember the call of the peacock in the jungle? Remember the rose with a damaged stalk lift its head again when I splinted it with a toothpick and sellotape just to see if it worked and it did.

Above all there was that moment when Alistair and I met and I knew that here was a person who was different from all the rest.

From being an Elder in the Scots Kirk where we had married, he no longer went to church; but no one who came to him in distress was ever refused.

It took enormous courage for him to take me home to Scotland at the end of the war and introduce me, from a distant island, to his people. Strength to give me strength living in a two-room flat with a semi-detached kitchen and a twice-a-week bath night. Strength after a hard day's work at his father's engineering works to go to night school and pass the four years course in two. To work in the largest engineering and commercial company in the island with a work force of 2,000, and to end up as its chairman. To cut away and start again in England as a consultant, and finally to (cut loose from there and) accept an appointment on the staff as an agro-engineer, at the World Bank, Nairobi, where we lived for twenty years.

He set his own horizons, thought of the broad principles first of any new project, then worked inside them, and reached out.

I go back to our first day in a Sri Lanka so changed that I could not recognize a single road. We stayed at the Hilton, for the small house that had belonged to my mother was far from ready for us. When, in Nairobi, the thought of what to get rid of, sell, or keep became too difficult in the limited time we had set ourselves, Alistair decided, "We take everything," for my sake; not his, for his instinct (rightly) would have disposed of all but the essentials. Instead he organised crates, cardboard boxes, called the packers, and our friends, and we all set about the enormous business of packing everything that had belonged in a two-storeyed house twice the size of our new No. 9.

Day after day we crouched over precious books – never mind if there were so many about Africa, I could not part with them. So many cookery books! Endless books on porcelain painting. "Take them, take what ever makes you happy." And so it went, he labelling everything in his meticulous handwriting, numbering the boxes. Then packers and friends came in for the rest, and we packed all day. The new Dutch couple who lived next door came in with a collapsible table, set it under a Jacaranda tree in the front courtyard, for we had had no table, linen or cutlery now and served a wonderful lunch… But back 'home' in Sri Lanka, our small house groaned at the seams, and a small room we could well have done with was lined with ceiling-high shelves where surplus boxes were placed temporarily.

We share a den now, our desks set diagonally across from each other where cross-currents deflect our voices and we have to shout. But he is there when I have computer trouble, which is almost every five minutes, or when I – or he - have a thousand other problems.

We sat at breakfast on the veranda this morning, and a slow wind sent drifts of crimson bougainvillea across one end of it.

"Alistair," I begin, tentatively. He looks up from his tray of fruit and coffee, his profile still sharp and clear, the bald dome of his head rising towards its silver crown.

"You are the most wonderful person I have ever known," I say. He thinks for a long time. "We've been a good team," he says.

For Alistair

Two shall be born the whole wide world apart,
And speak in different tongues, and have no thought
Each of his other's being; and have no heed;
And these, o'er unknown seas to unknown lands
Shall cross escaping wreck, defying death;
And all unconsciously shape every act to this one end;
But one day out of darkness they shall meet
And read life's meaning in each other's eyes.

- From Christine Wilson's Diary, 1949

To David Spenser and Vic Pemberton, thanks for their faith in me and to Suda and Smriti who got me out of many computer problems. My special thanks to my publishers who went far out of their way to help.